A Cruising Guide
to New Jersey Waters

A Cruising Guide to New Jersey Waters

⚓⚓⚓⚓⚓⚓⚓⚓⚓⚓⚓⚓⚓⚓⚓⚓⚓⚓⚓⚓⚓⚓⚓⚓⚓⚓⚓⚓

Revised Edition

Captain Donald Launer

Rutgers University Press

New Brunswick, New Jersey

Launer, Donald, 1926–
    A cruising guide to New Jersey waters / Donald Launer.
    p.   cm.
    Includes bibliographical references and index.
    ISBN 0-8135-3418-6 (alk. paper)
    1. Boats and boating—New Jersey—Guidebooks.   2. Waterways—New
Jersey—Guidebooks.   3. New Jersey—Guidebooks.   I. Title.
    GV776.N5L38 1995
    796.1'09749—dc20   95-8590
                                                                            CIP

A British Cataloging-in-Publication record for this book is available from the British Library

Manufactured in the United States of America

Affectionately dedicated to my wife, Elsie,
our children, Kathy and Tom,
and our grandchildren, Jennifer and Nancy
—outstanding crew members all

⚓ Contents

⚓ ⚓

General Information for Cruising

⚓ List of Illustrations and Tables

⚓ ⚓

In our schooner, *Delphinus*, anchored in a dense fog for thirty-six hours in
   Horseshoe Cove, inside Sandy Hook *206*
The author, Captain Don Launer *235*

$\mathcal{C}$harts

$\mathcal{T}$ables

⚓ Acknowledgments

*A*ny book such as this is a compilation of facts from many sources, local watermen, history books, government publications, and, primarily, my own experiences. I have been fortunate to have had the enthusiastic cooperation of many people and organizations in this endeavor. I would like to give credit to John Smath of Lanoka Harbor, who shared his expertise and experience from a lifetime on Raritan Bay and its tributaries and Andrew Wilner, New Jersey/New York Baykeeper, who provided insights on Sandy Hook Bay, Raritan Bay, Arthur Kill, Kill Van Kull, and Newark Bay. In this book I have used excerpts from some of the articles that I have written for Offshore, the northeast boating magazine, with the blessing of Herb Glick, publisher, as well as articles I have done for Good Old Boat Magazine.

Most of the photographs are my own. Keith Hamilton, of Studio 9 in Waretown, provided the aerial photographs, which give striking views of our shoreline. Other photographs are from Bill Schultz, Raritan Riverkeeper; Linda Riley of the Camden Aquarium; The Port Imperial Marina in Weehawkin; Jesse Lebovics, Rusty Kennedy and Tania Karpinich, of the Independence Seaport Museum in Philadelphia; George T. Schupp and Jeanne Covert of the Bayshore Discovery Project; and Trump Castle Associates.

The nautical charts are reproduced through the courtesy of the NOAA's National Ocean Service, a branch of the Department of Commerce.

If I have left anyone out, they are no less appreciated.

⚓ ⚓

A Cruising Guide
to New Jersey Waters

Introduction

Since the first edition of this book, there have been many changes affecting recreational boaters. Immediately after 9/11 sweeping new and important regulations were promulgated. Knowledge of these restrictions is of vital importance to all mariners. In addition, extensive changes in environmental restrictions on our waters must now be observed. These changes, coupled with the natural mutation of our waterways by wind and wave, as well as those man-made alterations of onshore facilities, make this new edition required reading for all those who use and enjoy our waters.

The fascination associated with traveling near or on the water seems to be imprinted on the human soul. Is it because we came from the sea and water still comprises most of our physical being, or is it because we know inherently that without water we couldn't exist? As small children we were drawn to streams, rivers, lakes, and oceans; and as adults we can still sit by the hour watching the breaking surf, a cascading waterfall, or a brook flowing through the woods. This appeal transcends our practical facade and touches our most romantic instincts. It manifests itself in the need to become a part of our environment, to be on or near the water, and to experience our most primal feelings.

For many people this translates into the desire to skipper their own boats—to replicate in some small way the voyages of their ancestors and to feel at one with the waters that comprise most of the surface of our planet.

This book, then, is a cruising guide designed to entice recreational boat owners in the northeast, whether of power or sail boats, to explore the navigable waters at their doorstep. It will also provide the armchair sailor with an opportunity to vicariously cruise the waters that border and lie within the Garden State. Included in the guide is information on navigation, anchorages, marinas, and weather, along with shoreside activities (such as waterside restaurants, sightseeing, historic locations, nature preserves, and entertainment), as well as safety tips—the type of information that is not available through government publications. Maritime adventures from the past are also chronicled for each area, so we will be cruising through history as well as geography.

When I say the book deals with the "navigable" waters of New Jersey, I use the term in both the legal and the more pragmatic sense—that is, those waters subject to tidal flow that are actually navigable. Although I have also spent thousands of hours on the nonnavigable waters of New Jersey in both my kayak and canoe (enjoying every moment), this guide will limit itself to ocean and tidal cruising.

With the exception of the 53-mile-long New York State land boundary on the north, New Jersey is almost completely surrounded by water, and a small boat can cruise more than 300 miles around the navigable perimeter of the state. The western boundary is the Delaware River, which is used recreationally by small boats along its entire length. It is only navigable below the falls at Trenton, and our trip up the Delaware will stop there.

Where I have named marinas and restaurants, it is because they are representative of the area. No endorsement is intended, and no inference should be made about those not mentioned. There will undoubtedly be readers who take exception to some of the ideas expressed—it has always been so. Herman Melville, when counseling a young American writer, lamented: "Pierre, . . . it is impossible to talk or to write, without throwing oneself helplessly open to criticism."

The material contained in the book is, however, to the best of my knowledge and at the time of writing, as accurate as possible; taking into account that our shoreline is constantly changing and that facilities on shore (marinas, restaurants, prices, and the like) are also open to change. Even as this book goes to press, I continue to explore in my schooner *Delphinus,* and in my dinghy or kayak. When new things are discovered, or errors are brought to light, they will, along with input from readers, contribute to better coverage in future editions.

Please note that the charts reproduced in this book are not intended to take the place of up-to-date NOAA government charts, tide tables, the *U.S. Coast Pilot,* or proper navigational practices. Indeed, we have made no attempt to reproduce the high level of detail in the original charts and have used the charts primarily to show the relationship between different waterways and land masses. The author and publisher disclaim any liability for loss or damage to persons or property that may occur as a result or interpretation of any information in this book.

Where there is a subjective opinion expressed, whether positive or negative, it is strictly my own. Those enamored with Atlantic City might be bored

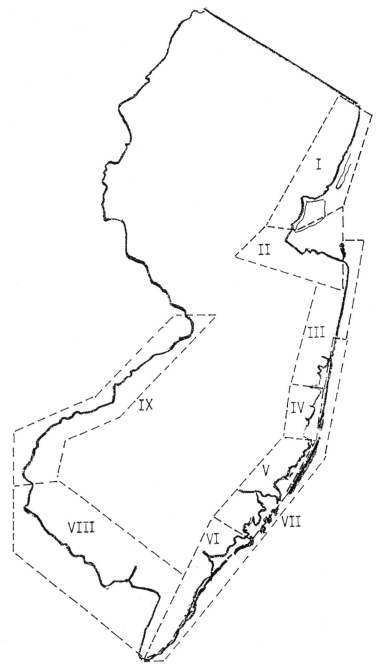

$\mathcal{C}$hart 1.1 Outline of New Jersey, indicating the areas covered by each of the nine chapters

spending a day treading for clams, and vice versa. Everyone's preferences and ideas are different, but New Jersey's waters offer a diversity that should satisfy all. My own views come from paddling, rowing, sailing, motoring, and swimming in New Jersey waters, a vocation as well as an avocation that continues nearly every day during the boating season.

Finally, I am not as interested in showing how the greatest distance can be covered in the least amount of time, but rather in the quality and safety of a life afloat. The enjoyment of being on board, savoring the delights of a cruising vacation in a safe manner, is my primary concern—those in a hurry should take a car or a plane.

We will begin our cruise at the northern limit of New Jersey's navigable waters, the Hudson River at the New Jersey–New York border, and follow the river south through New York Harbor, the Upper and Lower bays, and the Kill Van Kull and Arthur Kill between New Jersey and Staten Island.

We'll then explore Raritan Bay and Sandy Hook Bay, which are enclosed by Sandy Hook, the Atlantic Highlands, and Staten Island. While there we will look at the many tributaries that enter the bay from the south and west.

From Sandy Hook our cruise will take us south along the Atlantic coast to Manasquan Inlet, where the option of an inland passage again becomes available. In separate chapters we will take the offshore passage south as well as the inland route to Cape May.

The cruise through Delaware Bay, with side trips to the little rivers on the north, takes us to the Delaware River, where our course follows the river to the head of navigation at Trenton (chart 1.1).

At the end of most chapters there is a mileage table, showing distances in statute miles between locations mentioned in the text. In chapters 4, 5, and 6, which cover the intracoastal route, no mileage tables are provided since the distances along this intracoastal route are clearly marked on the charts.

I have sailed New Jersey's waters for more than seventy years and hope to continue doing so for many more. Thus, the recipe in this book includes a large measure of practical experience gained throughout a lifetime mixed with research and a dash of information garnered from those who have made a life on the water either of work or play.

It is unfortunately common for the older generation, while recalling time spent on our waters in their youth, to lament for yesteryear—for lost places, people, and lifestyles. Everyone likes to believe that his or her childhood belonged to a larger age of innocence, a time that no one will ever see again. But it is a form of conceit to believe that the golden age of New Jersey's water exists in memory and that within our lifetime (due to industrial, social, and bureaucratic upheaval), our waters have fallen from grace. It's a nostalgia

The author sailing his schooner, *Delphinus*, on Barnegat Bay

ill-used. Better to approach a day on the water with wide-eyed wonder and the heart of a child.

I'm sure that many New Jersey as well as out-of-state mariners view cruising New Jersey waters as an uninteresting prospect. To them I say, "Read on"; and to those approaching my vintage, my recommendation is: "Sail before sunset!"

Chapter One

The Hudson River at the New Jersey/New York State Line to New York's Lower Bay

*O*ur cruise of New Jersey's navigable waters begins on the northeastern corner of the state, the Hudson River at the New Jersey–New York line. At this point, exactly across the Hudson from Hastings-on-Hudson in Westchester, the state line extends to midriver.

It is 315 miles from the Hudson's source in the Adirondack Mountains of upstate New York to its mouth in New York Harbor between the Battery and Jersey City, and the river is navigable as far north as Troy. For most of its length, the Hudson River is entirely in New York State, but for the last 16 miles, until it merges with New York Harbor, the river shares its banks and waters with New Jersey.

From the headwaters of time, the Hudson has always held an attraction for the early inhabitants of North America, and radio carbon dating shows that humans lived in the Hudson River valley back at least as far as 4000 BC.

As we travel on the broad river from the New York border, we see to our west the soaring cliffs of the majestic Palisades, which rise up from the New Jersey shoreline and extend from just north of the New Jersey–New York state border to a point near the border of Bergen and Hudson counties. The Palisades were created 190 million years ago, when molten basalt erupted through the sandstone mantle and cooled into vertical columns that resembled the logs used to build traditional fortifications. The early pioneers dubbed them by the same name—palisades. We are fortunate that they have been preserved in their near-natural state by the Palisades Interstate Park Commission. In New Jersey, the Palisades Park runs for 10 miles, from the New York State line to a point just below the George Washington Bridge.

Wind patterns on the river are largely determined by the hills of the Pal-

The New Jersey Palisades along the Hudson River near Alpine. Armstrong's experimental FM tower rises above the trees

isades at the southern end and by the mountains on each bank further north, which channel the wind so that it travels along the axis of the river, blowing from either the north or south. Thus, cruising sailboats are either on a run or propelled by their engines, which sailors refer to as their iron wind. Those under sail who try tacking into an opposing wind and tide find this usually results in little or no net gain.

Few hazards exist for the small boat skipper on this stretch of the Hudson. Tides run about two knots at their peak, and there is ample water depth; midchannel is about forty feet. One must, however, be alert for debris in the water and to traffic, including large ships, tugs, barges, and ferries. It's wise to give large ships, especially tugboats with tows, the right of way without question; if there is any concern about their intentions they should be contacted on VHF Channel-13. Keep in mind that stopping or turning a large ship can take a mile or more to accomplish, and small craft under its bow are obscured from view. When a small boat in the vicinity of a large ship plans a change in direction, the move should be decisive, almost exaggerated, so there is no question about the course change or intention.

The waters of the Hudson River are making a substantial recovery from the major pollution problems of the 1950s. At that time manufacturing plants along its banks dumped waste chemicals into the water, and cities used it as a disposal site for raw sewage. Professional seafarers termed New York Harbor a "clean port," not because of the water purity, but rather because wood-boring worms, ship-worms, which destroy wooden ships, barges, and piers, were unable to thrive in the polluted waters. Finally, public awareness of the ever-increasing problem caused activism to replace complacency, and the federal, state, and city governments were prompted to adopt stringent environmental regulations. These new regulations and substantial penalties for failure to comply with them (along with watchdog citizen-advocacy groups on behalf of a clean environment), have made a noticeable change in the Hudson's waters, which are returning year by year from a legacy of environmental abuse.

Stewards of these waters—the eyes and ears for a clean environment—are now being established in estuaries, bays, and rivers throughout the United States and Canada; the Waterkeeper Alliance lists over 114 locations in all. Their missions are to protect, preserve, and restore the ecological integrity and productivity of the waters under their stewardship. In the New Jersey area these programs include: Hudson Riverkeeper; Delaware Riverkeeper; New York/New Jersey Baykeeper; Raritan Riverkeeper; Hackensack Riverkeeper; Passaic River Coalition; and the Great Egg Harbor Riverkeeper programs, among others.

Despite the Hudson's environmental problems, it is the only river in the eastern United States that still has the same aquatic wildlife as it did when the East Coast was first colonized by Europeans.

As we travel south along the New Jersey Palisades, we come to the first New Jersey marina in Alpine, nestled on a short skirt of land between the river and the foot of the cliffs. The Alpine Boat Basin is located about three and a half miles south of the New York border and is operated by the Palisades Interstate Park Commission. It has slips with electricity and water that are sheltered from the wash of Hudson River traffic, a gas dock, and picnic facilities. Before the Tappan Zee Bridge was built in 1955, a ferry service carried cars between this spot and Yonkers on the New York side. It was the only way across the river between the George Washington Bridge and Bear Mountain. At the Alpine marina there are two picturesque walking paths along the Hudson. Both the Shore Path at the base of the Palisades next to the river and the Long Path, which runs along the top of the cliffs, provide the walker or jogger with a spectacular setting.

South of Alpine a road called River Drive has been hewn into the face of the mountain. Trees arch across the road overhead; little brooks tumble down the face of the cliffs, and magnificent views of the river can be seen through the breaks in the trees. It is a delightful lane for a drive, a hike, or a bike ride (provided the bike has low gears).

At the top of the Palisades, at Alpine, a large tower with two horizontal crossarms can be seen for miles around. It is historically important in the field of broadcasting. In 1935, E. H. Armstrong, in a famous paper presented at the Institute of Radio Engineers, described his invention of FM (frequency modulation), and his first experiments in FM broadcasting were performed at this location.

More recently, the Alpine tower provided New York City's TV broadcast stations with an emergency antenna location for transmitting their programs to the New York metropolitan area. The antenna location for most of New York's TV stations had been atop the north tower of the World Trade Center, and on 9/11, when these buildings were destroyed, TV broadcasts to the metropolitan area went black. Within days, many New York stations set up emergency transmitters and antennas at the Alpine tower, providing coverage of the events that were changing Americans' sense of security forever. The tower was used for over a month, until more permanent locations were found.

Two miles before the George Washington Bridge, which links New Jersey and Manhattan Island, we find the Englewood Boat Basin, located on a narrow strip of land at the base of the Palisades. From the river, the sailboats' masts in the marina look like mere toothpicks against the lofty cliffs. The marina has protected slips and a fuel dock and is also operated by the Park Commission. Shore Path, along the Palisades, leads from this marina to the Alpine Marina and beyond. The Englewood Boat Basin is located directly across the river from the Spuyten Duyvil Creek, which separates the north end of Manhattan Island from the Bronx (the Bronx is named for Bronck's Farm, owned by Jonas Bronck, who farmed 500 acres there).

Few services currently exist for the small boat along Manhattan's waterfront. By contrast, every year there seem to be more and more marinas and small craft facilities being built along the river on the opposite shore in New Jersey.

Below the George Washington Bridge, which was completed in the depression year of 1931, the aura of being in a big city takes over, and the hustle and bustle on the water becomes more intense. On one side of the river are the natural cliffs of the New Jersey Palisades, on the other the artificial cliffs of Manhattan. There are marinas in the New Jersey town of Edgewater, between the bridge and the ferryboat restaurant *Binghamton*. Although it would be nice, there is no tie-up at the restaurant.

Manhattan, from this vantage point, puts on a benign face and seems to be the Emerald City of Oz—without dirt, crime, or traffic jams. The concrete monoliths create an incomparable panorama, and all lines in our view seem to be vertical, buildings reaching skyward.

This skyline changed dramatically on September 11, 2001, when two horrendous acts of terrorism brought down the twin towers of the World Trade Center. Shortly thereafter, as security concerns heightened, new boating restrictions were promulgated for all of our domestic waterways, with special restrictions for potential arenas of terrorism, such as New York Harbor. When these new restrictions were instituted they were termed "temporary," however it's probable that they will remain in effect for the foreseeable future.

One of the most important of these changes, for recreational boaters, concerns the security zones that have been established in the vicinity of naval vessels for all of the navigable waters of the United States. The new regulation, prompted by the possibility of suicide attacks on naval vessels by terrorists, establishes security zones around all of these ships. The first of these security zones requires all boats within 500 yards of a naval vessel to operate at the minimum speed necessary to maintain a safe course and to proceed as directed by the Official Patrol. Knowledge of this new restriction is vital for the recreational boater, since operating a boat at high speed in this restricted zone could be interpreted as a terrorist attack.

The second security zone around naval vessels prohibits any person or boat within 100 yards of a naval vessel, unless authorized by the Official Patrol. Violation of this provision not only could be prosecuted as a felony, punishable by fine of $250,000 and six months in jail, but in addition, a naval vessel could respond with deadly force against an unauthorized boat encroaching on these restricted areas—a possible "shoot now and ask questions later" scenario. Boats are also not allowed within 100 yards of an anchored or moored Coast Guard vessel. In areas where the narrow waterway does not allow these stipulated clearances, the small boat skipper must contact the ship or the Official Patrol on Ch-16 for permission to pass within the 100 yard restricted area.

These security zones are taken very seriously. Senator John Breaux (D-LA) expressed this concern: "I'm convinced that the greatest security threats to ports isn't from a terrorist taking over a ship, but something more like what happened to the USS *Cole*." (The USS *Cole* was nearly sunk by suicide bombers aboard an open runabout in Yemen in 2001.)

The Office of Homeland Security now requires that every major port has its own security plan. Several special security zones have been established in the greater New York Harbor area. Entry into these restricted areas is punishable by a fine of up to $50,000, five years imprisonment, or both. These restricted zones include the waters of Newark Bay west of the main channel;

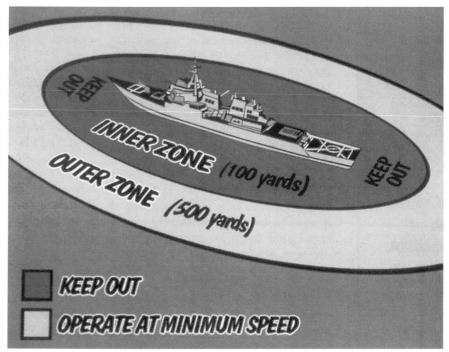

Chart 1.2 The security zone around naval vessels

within 150 yards of Liberty or Ellis Islands; within 25 yards of all bridge piers or abutments, overhead power cables, and tunnel ventilators; within 125 yards of the Manhattan shoreline near the United Nations; within 175 yards of the shorelines at the Queensboro Bridge; within 100 yards of all anchored or moored Coast Guard vessels; the waters close to piers 84–96; all waters of the Military and Global Marine Terminals of the New Jersey Pier Head Channel; and within 100 yards of any passenger ship, or any barge carrying bulk petroleum or chemicals.

Captain Scott Evans of the Coast Guard stresses that: "If you drop an anchor to go fishing near a bridge, you can probably expect to be boarded."

In Sandy Hook Bay there has always been a restricted area around the Naval Weapons Station Earle Piers (see chapter 2). This restricted area has been expanded beyond the area shown on the charts.

Since these security regulations are constantly being revised, boaters should check the latest *Local Notice to Mariners,* the weekly publication of the U.S. Department of Homeland Security/U.S. Coast Guard. In addition, recreational boaters should check their charts meticulously when transiting these waters to avoid these restricted areas. They should also be on the lookout for patrol vessels and continuously monitor VHF Ch-16 for any possible instructions.

With 95,000 miles of coastline to patrol, the U.S. Coast Guard encourages the recreational boater to assist in becoming their "eyes and ears." A boater can report any suspicious activity by calling 911 or *CG on their cell phone, or call the Coast Guard on VHF Ch-16.

As we continue down the Hudson we see that the New Jersey skyline across the river is being revitalized with marinas, luxury apartments, and town houses. Typical of this rebirth are two marinas in Weehawken. (History buffs will remember that Weehawken was the site of the famous duel between Alexander Hamilton and Aaron Burr, in which Hamilton was mortally wounded.) The name Weehawken is an American Indian name, meaning "rows of trees"; it referred to the vertical rock columns of the Palisades that resembled the edge of a forest.

Marinas in Weehawken give easy access to Manhattan. One of these is the 350-acre Port Imperial Marina. It is a full service marina, offering facilities for transients: fuel, boat repairs, a ship's store, hauling and engine parts, a restaurant, and the FerryBus to Manhattan. Call the marina on VHF Ch-9, Ch-16, or Ch-88A. The marina advertises: "Just five blocks and a ferry ride from your favorite Broadway show." Arthur's Landing Restaurant, located there, offers a pre-theater dining package that includes a complimentary round-trip ferry service and connecting shuttle bus to and from the New York theater district.

At Pier-86, at the west end of Manhattan's 46th Street, is the USS *Intrepid* Sea-Air-Space Museum complex (Manhattan pier numbers are the street numbers plus forty). On the south side of Pier-86 is the aircraft carrier USS *Intrepid*, which was launched in 1943; and on the north side are the submarine USS *Growler*; and the supersonic Concorde, which was brought in by barge from Kennedy Airport in November 2003. The museum complex is also home

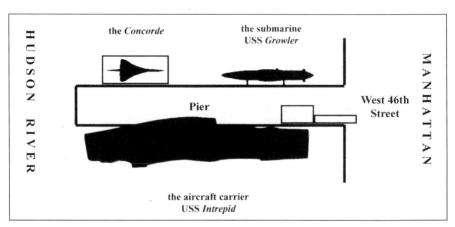

Chart 1.3 The USS *Intrepid* Sea-Air-Space Museum complex (2004 display configuration)

to a large variety of historic military aircraft and is constantly acquiring new exhibits. To accommodate these displays, the museum is currently expanding its territory along the Hudson River waterfront. The destroyer USS *Edson*, whose space along the pier was displaced by the Concorde, will be part of this expanded exhibit. The museum, which has been declared a National Historic Landmark, is a private nonprofit institution that draws over 600,000 visitors annually, and is a must-see attraction. It can be easily reached using Manhattan transportation as well as from New Jersey by ferry and a short walk.

Farther south along Manhattan's Hudson River waterfront (between 17th and 23rd streets) the Chelsea Piers project, on four 600-foot piers, provides Manhattan's waterfront with a whole range of recreational options. The piers and terminal buildings were originally built for passenger liner traffic in 1910.

Whenever I pass lower Manhattan by boat, I recall my father telling me of his first visit to New York City as a child in the late 1890s. In those days the soaring bowsprits of great sailing vessels from all over the world thrust across the crowded waterfront. The forest of masts, the rigging whistling in the wind, and the noise of the dock carts rattling over the cobblestones has now been

In Weehawken, looking across the Hudson at the Empire State Building in Manhattan, with Port Imperial Marina in the foreground (photo courtesy of J. B. Grant and Port Imperial Marina)

replaced with the sound of cars and sirens from the express highway that runs beside the river.

The Port of New York handled more tonnage than any other port in the world until 1900. Now, many of the piers on the Hudson along Manhattan Island have fallen into disrepair, while most of the major commercial shipping vessels—tankers, freighters, and container ships—have moved their base of operations to the New Jersey ports off Newark Bay, like Port Newark and Port Elizabeth, or to those along the Arthur Kill, which separates New Jersey and Staten Island.

During the 1800s, Hoboken, across the river from lower Manhattan, was a vacation spot for New Yorkers, who went there on weekends and holidays, considering it a visit to the country. The short ferry ride took them into the Elysian Fields in Hoboken (then a bucolic setting with woods and rolling lawns), where the adults could spend the day relaxing under the trees while the children frolicked until the picnic lunch was ready. It was here that a diamond was set up on the grass and the first modern baseball game was played in 1845.

South of Jersey City, we enter the Upper New York Bay, which is bounded by Manhattan on the north, New Jersey on the west, Brooklyn on the east, and Staten Island and the Narrows to the south (chart 1.4). When we cruise through the harbor, I always keep a sharp lookout for debris in the water, large ship traffic, and the ferries that charge back and forth from Manhattan to Staten Island, Liberty Island, Governor's Island, Ellis Island, and Jersey City. I never make any naive or theoretical assumptions about who has the right of way—basic logic tells me that they do.

Legendary Ellis Island, with its Moorish architecture, is just a few hundred yards off the New Jersey shore and connected to it by a bridge that can only be used by park rangers and employees. This bridge also supplies the utilities to the island. When passing the island, watch out for the ferries entering or leaving, and observe the new security zone.

By now, as we pass Ellis Island, all eyes on board are directed toward the Statue of Liberty, three-quarters of a nautical mile to our south on Liberty Island, and we wish we had more than one pair of binoculars. The 305-foot monument, which faces southeast to welcome those entering the harbor through the Narrows, was completely refurbished in 1986 and now looks pristine. There are submerged rocks and pilings close to the shore at the north, east, and south sides of the island, but small boats can safely pass within a couple of hundred yards to the east. Again, be sure to keep a watchful eye out for ferry traffic and observe the security restricted area around the island. The only access to Liberty Island is by ferries that leave either from Manhattan; from

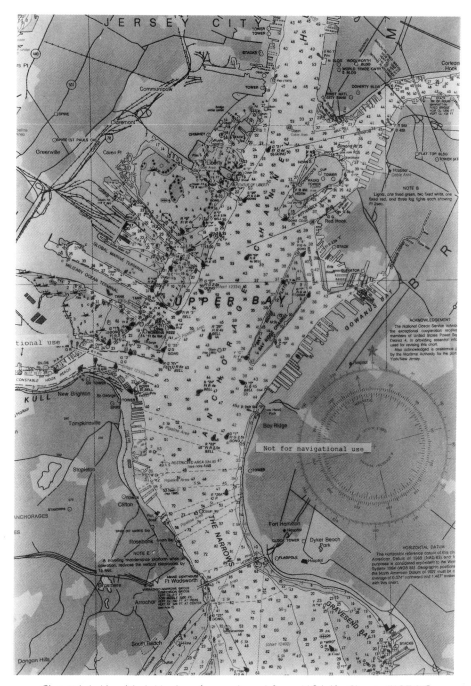

*C*hart 1.4 New York Harbor (reproduced from NOAA's Chart #12327)

The Statue of Liberty in New York Harbor

New Jersey's Liberty State Park, 600 yards to the west; or from Hoboken. These ferries bring throngs of visitors, over a million a year, to the island.

We occasionally see some buoys in the water near Liberty Island that look like lobster-pot buoys, and that's because lobsters are being caught here; a tangible testament to the improving water quality.

Luckily we haven't forgotten to bring cameras along, since the sights in all directions from this vantage point are spectacular. We now turn east across New York Harbor toward the southern tip of Manhattan, which brings us to the confluence of the East River and the Hudson River at the Battery. (The Battery was named for the battery of ninety-two cannon that the British placed there in 1693 to defend against French attacks.) Along the Manhattan shoreline of the East River is the picturesque South Street Seaport, with the spider web cables of the Brooklyn Bridge just beyond. The East River gives the boater access to Long Island Sound and beyond. Tidal flow can be swift here at the height of a tide change, and auxiliary sailboats, trawlers, or other displacement hulls are well advised to wait for either a favorable tidal flow or slack tide.

At the South Street Seaport docks, which are just south of the historic Brooklyn Bridge, there is a wonderful collection of old ships. This largest privately owned collection of historic ships in the United States (in tonnage) includes the *Wavertree,* a three-masted ship built in 1885; the 1911 four-masted

South Street Seaport

The Brooklyn Bridge

barque *Peking*; the first Ambrose lightship, built in 1908; and the recently acquired *Helen McAllister*, whose keel was laid in 1900. In addition are the seaport's training vessels, which include the 1885 cargo schooner *Pioneer* that takes passengers on daily trips around New York Harbor; the *Lettie G. Howard*, a restored oysterer; and the *W. O. Decker*, which was built in 1930.

The preservation, restoration, and development of South Street Seaport began uncertainly in 1967. (Finally, the Rouse Company, whose wizardry was responsible for Baltimore's Inner Harbor and for Boston's Quincy Market, provided the impetus.) South Street, named because this part of Manhattan faces south, now provides a mosaic of diversions. Visitors have an unforgettable glimpse of the past in this twelve-square-block historic district. In the atmosphere of the eighteenth and nineteenth centuries one will find dock-side concerts, street musicians, jugglers, shops, restaurants, and bookstores, located along the stone-paved streets. The South Street Seaport's museum is crammed with exhibits and galleries, and hosts living history and educational programs for both children and adults.

When we leave the East River, heading across the harbor toward the Verrazano Bridge, we usually take the channel between Governors Island and Brooklyn; there is less traffic there and the route is slightly shorter. Governor's

Island was the home base in New York Harbor for the U.S. Coast Guard for many decades.

The Verrazano Bridge joins the boroughs of Brooklyn and Staten Island and vaults across the hourglass waist of the Narrows, which separates New York's upper and lower bays. The Lower Bay, to the south of the Narrows, is part of the larger bay, which is also comprised of Sandy Hook Bay and Raritan Bay. These are not separate bays, as such, but actually sections of the same body of water, joined by indefinite boundaries. Sandy Hook Bay is the area to the southeast of the Lower Bay, and Raritan Bay is the area to the southwest.

On the north side of Staten Island, as we head south toward the Verrazano, the Kill Van Kull branches off the harbor to the west. This waterway, which is the boundary between New Jersey and Staten Island, New York, connects with the Arthur Kill and is an optional route to Raritan Bay. It also provides an entrance into Newark Bay, and ultimately the Passaic and Hackensack rivers that flow north into the northern New Jersey suburbs. (This alternate route will be discussed later in this chapter.)

When heading through the Narrows, one can encounter an annoying sea that can develop against an opposing wind and tide. In addition, the steel framework of the Verrazano Bridge (as with most large bridges) can affect the compass or cause a course change when the boat is under autopilot. Also, water boundary layers of temperature called thermoclines below the boat can cause the depth-sounder to show only a few feet; but be assured, the depth is more than adequate.

The graceful Verrazano Narrows Bridge is nearly a mile long. A civil engineer once told me that the towers of the Verrazano Bridge are vertical but are not parallel. As I was pondering this, he explained, "Since the support towers are so far apart, there's a slight curvature of the earth between them."

The Verrazano Bridge across the Narrows was named after the first European explorer to discover and record the existence of this estuary. Approximately seventy-five years after Columbus tried to reach Cathay by sailing west, Florentine navigator Giovani da Verrazano made another attempt farther north on the American continent, sailing under the French flag. He first sighted the coast near Cape Fear, North Carolina. He headed south for a while but, nervous about the potential threat from Spanish ships, decided to explore north along the coast. Inexplicably, he entirely missed the vast entrances to the Chesapeake and Delaware bays, finally dropping anchor in Sandy Hook Bay. Due to contrary winds and tides, as well as the uncertainty of depths, the ship's boat was rowed up through the Narrows on an exploration of New York Harbor and the lower Hudson River. Verrazano then returned to France without ever giving a name to either the bay or river.

It wasn't until 1609 that the Hudson River was given the name that it currently holds. In September of that year, Henry Hudson's clumsy little Dutch craft *De Halve Maen,* or *The Half Moon,* with a favorable breeze, began a three week exploration of the river north of the Narrows. After crossing the Upper Bay *The Half Moon* passed an island of rocky hills and forests, where tangled vines clung to the trees and wolves and deer moved through the underbrush. The Canarsie Indian tribe's name for this island was Mana-hatin. By the time Hudson's ship reached the navigable limits of the Hudson, 150 miles from the ocean, it had finally become apparent that this was not the northwest passage to Cathay, but only a river, and they turned southward again from Castle Island, near the present city of Albany. As the Native Americans along the shore watched the ships, they surely didn't realize that their lives were about to change forever.

The Native Americans' prefix "Mana," meant "by the water," and we not only find this prefix for Mana-hatan but also in the names of towns along the New Jersey shore, such as Manahawkin, and Manasquan.

Navigation from the Verrazano, across the bay to the New Jersey shoreline, as well as trips up the tidal tributaries of Sandy Hook Bay and Raritan Bay are explored in chapter 2, but first let's look at the alternate route from New York Harbor to Raritan Bay, the Kill Van Kull and Arthur Kill.

*T*he Kill Van Kull and Arthur Kill separate Staten Island from New Jersey. Staten Island is a corruption of the original Dutch name, Staaten Eylandt, named for the States General at that time. In the 1600s both New York and New Jersey claimed Staten Island as their own. To settle the dispute it was finally agreed that New York could have all of the islands in the harbor that could be circumnavigated by sailboat within 24 hours. New Jersey was sure to obtain Staten Island since sailboats of that era had trouble going to windward, which would cause difficulties when trying to make the passage through the narrow waters to the north and west of the island. New York gave Captain Charles Billop and his sloop *Bently* the task. By today's standards the *Bently* looked like an awkward and inefficient little craft; but, through skillful short-tacking and playing the tides, Captain Billop accomplished the impossible, and the Borough of Richmond (Staten Island) became a part of New York City.

Captain Billop was rewarded with lands and a manor house at Tottenville on the island he won for New York. More than one hundred years later his home, which was built in 1668, again found a niche in history when it became the site of the first peace negotiations that led to the end of the American Revolution.

The Kill Van Kull takes the nautical nomad to the industrial waterways of

New Jersey seldom visited by recreational boaters, but this doesn't mean the trip is hazardous or devoid of interest. The Kill Van Kull and northern Arthur Kill are the major channels for bulk, containerized, and petroleum cargo in New York Harbor. So, we'll be sharing the traffic lanes with ships that are constricted to the channel and are unable to stop or turn easily; it's our responsibility to stay out of the way. Although these waters have long been avoided by the recreational boater due to debris and pollution, the stringent enforcement of environmental regulations has rendered the water quality better than it has been any time in the last seventy-five years. Many manufacturing and petroleum plants that found an economic advantage in dumping their waste products in these waters have closed down or moved, and the present industries along the waterfront have been obliged to reduce their pollution to nearly zero.

When heading west up the Kill Van Kull from New York Harbor, Bayonne, New Jersey, is on our north and Staten Island is to our south (chart 1.5). They are joined by the Bayonne Bridge. With a span of 1,652 feet, it was the longest steel archbridge in the world when it was built, but a few years later exactly the same type of bridge was built across the harbor in Sydney, Australia. That one was six inches longer.

Immediately past this bridge, the waterway separates. The channel to the north leads into Newark Bay, which is the route of the container ships that use the docks at Port Elizabeth and Port Newark.

Boat traffic on the Kill Van Kull

The Bayonne Bridge across the Kill Van Kull

Surprisingly, Newark Bay, long a victim of pollution and overindustrialization, supports a large population of blue-claw crabs, clams, and fish. The blue crabs are some of the biggest on the eastern seaboard (perhaps because catching them is prohibited), and recently when the Marine Fisheries put in a net for a striped bass survey, the net was so heavy with bass it couldn't be hoisted on board. In Newark Bay we must reiterate the current prohibition from transiting the restricted areas in these waters.

At the north end of Newark Bay, after passing beneath the Pulaski Highway and beyond the highway fixed bridge and the Conrail lift bridge, one comes to the confluence of the Passaic and Hackensack rivers. The Passaic River, the second longest river within New Jersey (next to the Raritan), has its origins in the Great Swamp. It is navigable by small boat all the way to the town of Passaic, although crossed by numerous fixed, swing, lift, and bascule bridges. In 1881, one of the first successful submarines was launched into the Passaic River at Paterson by its inventor, John Holland. Surprisingly, a hundred years ago the Passaic River was also an important link in freight commerce between New York City and Pennsylvania.

America was canal crazy in the 1800s. In the northeast alone, more than four thousand miles of canals were built. When a link from New York City to the coal- and iron-producing areas of eastern Pennsylvania was proposed, the Morris Canal went on the drawing boards. A survey of the terrain between

Looking north up Newark Bay toward the Pulaski Skyway

New York Harbor and the Lehigh River of Pennsylvania, a 55-mile distance as the crow flies, showed that the proposed canal route would be 102 miles. The route would proceed from New York Harbor, through the Kill Van Kull into Newark Bay, then up the Passaic River to Little Falls. A canal would then be dug to the south end of Lake Hopatcong, and from there it would lead southwest to the Delaware River, just opposite the Lehigh River and south of Easton, Pennsylvania, and Phillipsburg, New Jersey. Since the Delaware River is not navigable to either the north or the south at this point because of rapids every few miles, the Morris Canal would only be useful as a connection to the Lehigh Valley coal mines. The proposed route meant raising the barges 914 feet over the mountains, which was to be done not through the use of locks, but on dry land. To accomplish the task, twenty-three inclined planes with tracks would be needed. In the spring of 1832, the Morris Canal opened. Years later the eastern end of the canal was extended with a cut through Bayonne and Jersey City, providing an even more direct route.

The allure of canals was brief, however, and the 4-mile-an-hour canal traffic finally succumbed to the steam locomotive. After 1860 the Morris Canal started into a decline that finally ended in 1924 when it was abandoned.

The Hackensack River, which branches off Newark Bay to the northeast, is navigable by boat as far as the town of Hackensack, although also crossed by a variety of fixed bridges and drawbridges. The Hackensack River begins in

*C*hart 1.5 Kill Van Kull, Newark Bay, and northern Arthur Kill (reproduced from NOAA's Chart #12327)

the hills of New York State, and in its lower reaches the banks of the river are a mixture of wetlands and industry. Unfortunately, water quality in the Hackensack is poor, containing metals, PCBs, dioxins, bacteria, and petroleum. Paradoxically, as with Newark Bay, the Hackensack abounds with marine life. It is common to see the banks of the Hackensack crowded with fishermen and crabbers, although the fishing advisory says there should be no taking of crabs or of stripers.

Skippers with large boats who would like to take a trip up the Hackensack and anticipate opening bridges along the way may well want to reconsider. Most of the bridges have restricted opening hours. Some bridges require a one-hour notice and others require as much as an eight-hour notice. The river also has a great deal of commercial traffic, as barges and tugboats ply the waters all the way to the head of navigation at Hackensack, where there is an oil terminal.

During the 1600s the waterways of this area were the realm of pirates who preyed on the commerce of Hoboken, Jersey City, and New York City both by land and by sea. In 1695 the governor of New York, Edward Fletcher, who was perfectly willing to take bribes from the pirates and look the other way, was replaced by the Earl of Bellomont, who arrived from England with orders to clean up the cutthroats. The pirates retreated up the Hackensack River and continued their rampages. Finally, in 1797, the citizens had had enough and formed a vigilante group, with volunteers from Bergen County and from New York City, determined to eliminate the pirates once and for all. Outnumbered, the pirates disappeared into the undergrowth of the meadowlands. This area was set afire. The south wind fanned the flames and drove the pirates up to Rutherford, into the arms of vigilantes, ending the one-hundred-year reign of the Hackensack pirates.

At the juncture of the Kill Van Kull, Arthur Kill, and the channels into Newark Bay, be sure not to short-cut the channels between Newark Bay and the Arthur Kill near Shooters Island, where there is a submerged dike and very shallow water. In recent years Shooters Island, to the south, has developed into a wildlife sanctuary.

Along the Arthur Kill derelict barges and old ships are in the tidal flats off-channel, so search the surface of the water for debris. Each year more of these derelicts are being removed, but it's a slow process. These waters are also home to commercial shipyards and dry-docks.

Traveling down the Arthur Kill (*kill* is a Dutch word that means channel, stream, creek, or river) the shoreline is a mass of refineries, storage tanks, railroad tracks, and docks and carries an unmistakable odor of petrochemicals, the same smell that permeates this area along the New Jersey

A ships' graveyard off the Arthur Kill

Turnpike, only a half-mile to our west. But how can we complain when the very boat we're traveling in makes use of these products, both as a means of propulsion and as the principle component in the manufacture of the fiberglass hull.

As we head south on the Arthur Kill we pass beneath a railroad bridge. Three hundred yards farther south of the railroad bridge is the Goethals Bridge, a high, arching, cantilevered structure. The bridge was named for George Washington Goethal, the chief consulting engineer for the Port Authority of New York and New Jersey, who gained fame when he completed the Panama Canal after the French abandoned the project.

As we proceed down the Arthur Kill, we need to be aware of a buoy reversal. When we entered the Kill Van Kull from New York Harbor, we were going inland and the buoys were *red, right, returning,* as would be expected. But as we proceed down the Arthur Kill, we are now heading out to sea again, and although proper, this sudden buoy reversal can be a source of confusion. Double-check the charts.

Just before the Rahway River branches off to the west we pass Pralls Island, a bird sanctuary. Although in an unlikely location, it sports an ever-increasing population of gulls and herons, who share the shoreline with factories and oil refineries. Pralls Island is one of three islands on the Arthur Kill that supports the return of ospreys to the area. In fact the whole Raritan Bay region is seeing and increase in nesting ospreys each year—testament to an improving environment.

The Rahway River, which branches off into the New Jersey suburbs, is navigable well inland and is noted for spectacular fishing. Because of an accumulation of bottom sediments such as metals, PCBs, dioxin, and other toxins, fish taken here should be eaten sparingly and with the fatty tissues removed, or not at all. Unfortunately there are many people in the metropolitan area who fish for sustenance, and fish taken from contaminated streams such as this present a potential source of health problems.

Shoal-draft craft can navigate the river up to the Rahway Yacht Club, a club near the head of navigation. From the club it is a short walk to restaurants and a variety of stores.

As we continue south on the Arthur Kill, it takes a sharp turn to the west (chart 1.6). On the Staten Island side of this bend is a ships' graveyard, and just beyond the bend is an electric generating plant on the New Jersey shore. South of this point the waterway takes on a less industrial and more residential atmosphere.

New Jersey's navigable waters reveal great contrasts, and none more so than the entrance to the picturesque little stream of Smith Creek, which branches off the Arthur Kill amidst oil tanks, large ships, and a PSE&G generating plant. Smith Creek, on the New Jersey shore, has a marked entrance and

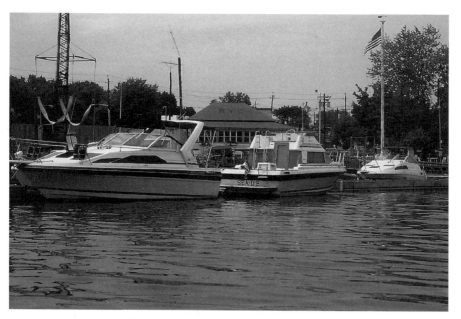

The Rahway Yacht Club on the Rahway River

An oil tanker at dock on the Arthur Kill. Note the floats in the water surrounding the ship. These are in place whenever loading or unloading operations take place, to contain any possible oil spill.

Smiths Creek off Arthur Kill

*C*hart 1.6 Southern Arthur Kill (reproduced from NOAA's Chart # 12327)

Looking north at the Outerbridge Crossing, on southern Arthur Kill

The Staten Island train terminal and remains of the old ferry slip south of the Outerbridge Crossing

The Perth Amboy Yacht Club on the Arthur Kill near Raritan Bay

Launching ramp and park on the Arthur Kill in Perth Amboy

Staten Island homes on the shore of the lower Arthur Kill

The Perth Amboy shoreline bordering the Arthur Kill

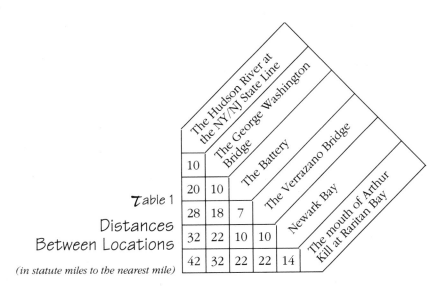

Table 1

Distances Between Locations

(in statute miles to the nearest mile)

The Hudson River at the NY/NJ State Line	The George Washington Bridge	The Battery	The Verrazano Bridge	Newark Bay	The mouth of Arthur Kill at Raritan Bay
10					
20	10				
28	18	7			
32	22	10	10		
42	32	22	22	14	

is easily navigable. Up the stream is a marina serving small craft, which offers slips for transients, fuel, ice, package goods, repairs, and winter storage. On the west side of the creek there are boat slips all along the shore, while on the east there are woods and marshlands. The ambiance is more reminiscent of a stream on the eastern shore of the Chesapeake than a waterway in the most densely populated area in the United States. Even if no services or supplies are required, a side trip a little way up the creek is enough to elicit exclamations from all aboard.

Farther south on the Arthur Kill there is another high cantilevered bridge, the Outerbridge Crossing, a major highway artery between New Jersey and Staten Island. Most people assume that the Outerbridge Crossing was named because it is the most outer, or seaward, of the bridges connecting New Jersey and New York. This is only partially true. At the time the bridge was being constructed the Port Authority of New York and New Jersey was just being organized, and the "father of the Port Authority" was an administrator named Eugenius Harvey Outerbridge. In 1926, when the new bridge across the Arthur Kill was opened, the Port Authority, in a spirit of a pun, named the new bridge the Outerbridge Crossing.

Just below the Outerbridge Crossing, on the Staten Island shore, there are marinas offering small craft services, including repairs. Beyond the marinas there is a train yard that can be seen from the water, with the remains of an old ferry pier next to it. In years past, people from Manhattan could take the ferry to Staten Island, the train to this point, another ferry across the Arthur Kill, and finally a train to the New Jersey shore or to destinations farther west.

As we continue south on the Arthur Kill, we see large expensive residential homes that dot the shoreline on Staten Island. South of the Outerbridge Crossing on the New Jersey shore, as we approach Raritan Bay, is the Armory Restaurant, a brick building near the new Municipal Marina. Just beyond that we pass the Perth Amboy Yacht Club, where sailboat races are held on summer weekends. The yacht club has guest moorings and reciprocal privileges. Just south of the yacht club, on the southeastern tip of Perth Amboy, where the Arthur Kill joins Raritan Bay, there is an attractive new town park along the waterfront.

While taking my first trip through the kills around Staten Island, I found it so interesting that I kept wondering why I had never done it before. Although not on the itinerary of most cruising boaters, this exploration is well worth taking at least once. It provides a whole new insight into the industrial waterways of New Jersey that lie in the shadow of the Big Apple. The trip is a panorama of contrasts and definitely not what your preconceived notions would lead you to expect.

Chapter Two

The Lower Bay, Sandy Hook Bay, Raritan Bay, and Their Tributaries

For most cruising skippers Sandy Hook Bay and Raritan Bay are not usually considered destinations. But those who rush on are missing a fascinating cruising locale right at their doorstep.

Passing south through the Narrows, which is spanned by the Verrazano Bridge, we find ourselves in New York's Lower Bay. On a clear day we can see Sandy Hook and the Highlands of New Jersey in the distance. The north tip of the hook is only 9 miles away and the highlands five miles further south.

In the 1930s a project to build a bridge across the Narrows was on the verge of fruition, but with the likelihood of war in Europe, it was shelved. The fear was that a bridge across the Narrows could be the target of shelling or sabotage, and if it collapsed into the water, it could effectively close off the Port of New York, a port vital to any war effort. The bridge across the Narrows was not built until the 1960s.

When war did come to our shores German U-boats operated virtually unimpeded along the Atlantic Coast of North America in Germany's Operation Paukenschlag, under the command of Admiral Karl Donitz. During that brief period more than four hundred Allied ships were sent to the bottom of the ocean between Canada and Panama—a greater catastrophe in the loss of lives and of ship tonnage than the attack on Pearl Harbor. Virtually no counter-measures were taken. In fact, coastal hotel and amusement-park lights were left on so the tourist business would not suffer; the lights created perfect silhouettes of the cargo ships and tankers and were an immense aid to German U-boats' activity. Even lighthouses, navigation buoys, and ships displayed their normal lights.

There was also the very real possibility that U-boats would enter New York Harbor through the Narrows to destroy the convoys forming there. To counter this, a submarine net was set up south of where the Verrazano Bridge now stands. It stretched from tiny Swinburne Island, west of the main channel, across to Coney Island. This net protected the troopships, tankers, and cargo ships inside New York Harbor from attack.

My most memorable trip through the Narrows, in the days before the Verrazano Bridge existed, took place on a troopship returning from Europe after World War II. As we entered New York Harbor, we saw, to our right, a huge sign laid out on the grassy slopes of Brooklyn Heights; it said: "Welcome Home." To our left stood the Statue of Liberty, with her arm raised in salutation. Every GI on board had tears in his eyes—we were finally home. Coincidentally, my father had made that same entrance into New York Harbor after World War I twenty-five years earlier. I'm thankful that our son, Tom, was not obliged to repeat the tradition.

From the Narrows, on a clear day, we can see New Jersey's Highlands and Sandy Hook, forming the southeast boundary of Sandy Hook Bay. The trip from the Narrows to Sandy Hook poses no special problems when there is adequate visibility and sea conditions are satisfactory. We need to be aware, however, that the buoyed channels crisscrossing the bay are used by major shipping. Depths required by recreational boats are good almost everywhere, so traveling outside the marked channels is not only acceptable, but it keeps us out of the heavy commercial shipping lanes. Crossing the bay on a foggy day is quite another story. Once, my wife, Elsie, and I, under pressure of a schedule, decided to cross in a heavy fog. Traveling with Loran but no radar, we had only gone a few hundred yards when we heard the rumble of massive engines approaching, and a tug pushing a barge emerged from the mist on a parallel coarse, about fifty feet away. We decided to turn back and wait until the fog cleared. Those using radar, and confident of their skills, may elect to do otherwise.

When strong and prolonged winds are blowing from the east or southeast, the trip between the Narrows and Sandy Hook can be very rough, and even dangerous, for a small open boat. Under these circumstances there is always the option of using the kills around the west side of Staten Island (the alternate route that was described in chapter 1).

These waters south of New York City are where New York and New Jersey's largest rivers meet the Atlantic Ocean. The harbor estuary is an oasis of life that has suffered greatly from urbanization and industrialization. In 1990 the American Littoral Society established the "Baykeeper" program to provide a unified voice to the advocacy groups of marine and shore protection and to seek solutions to the environmental problems of the estuary.

Andrew Wilner, the baykeeper for the New Jersey/New York Harbor,

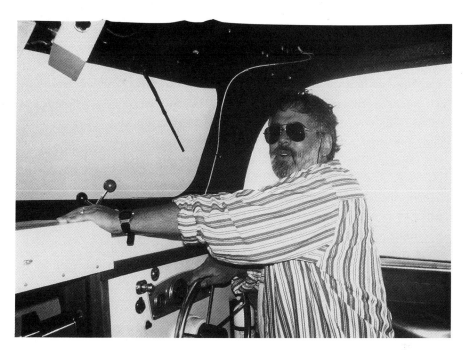

The New Jersey/New York Baykeeper, on Raritan Bay (photos courtesy of Bill Schultz, Baykeeper Auxiliary)

patrols these waters. He tracks down sources of litter, liquid poisons, and slicks of chemicals or oils that escape from ships or unseen pipes, He is the spokesperson and conscience of the harbor estuary who, along with a network of volunteers from all walks of life, monitors water quality parameters every two weeks at strategic locations and watches for polluters of these beleaguered waters. The baykeepers are the vanguard in the peaceful citizens' battle against water pollution, and they deserve the thanks of all who have concern for the environment. They offer a tangible ray of hope for reversing more than two hundred years' worth of damage to this fragile marine ecosystem.

Surprisingly, the major source of pollution in these waters now is not from "point-source" pollution, that is, from industries or sewage disposal. Instead, the major culprit is "non-point-source" or pollution from lawn chemicals, farms, road runoff, and the like. Cindy Zipf, executive director of Clean Ocean Action, aptly described this as "pointless pollution."

New restrictions on ocean dumping have gone a long way toward ameliorating the problem, and New York sewage sludge, which was once dumped offshore, is now shipped by railroad tank cars to farms in Texas for use as fertilizer.

One of the parameters used to judge water quality, or water that will support marine life, is dissolved oxygen. In the 1950s and 1960s a simple test for dissolved oxygen entailed taking a healthy fish, putting it in the bay's waters, and timing how many seconds it would take the fish to die. But since the 1976 Federal Clean Waters Act, reduced pollution in all our waters has resulted in a resurgence of marine life—including marine borers that feed on wooden bulkheads, wharves, docks, and wood boats. The irony of having cleaner waters is that all wood in contact with the water is now being attacked by these cellulose-eaters at an alarming rate. When waterways were badly polluted, substandard treated wood could last a deceptively long time—there weren't many wood-destroying organisms living in the polluted water. As water was cleaned up, the lack of proper wood treatment became more obvious; wood-destroying organisms became more prevalent and insufficiently protected wood didn't last long.

With the increased water purity, all marine life is proliferating, even the species we would rather do without. As with most marine life forms, the abundance of wood-eating organisms in the water is cyclical, and can depend on water quality, salinity, predators, and other wide-ranging influences.

In the era before steel, aluminum, or fiberglass boats, when all ships were made of wood, the shipworm was a scourge that could result in your ship literally sinking from under you. Frequently ships' crews unexpectedly had to abandon their craft because it was too rotten to sail any farther—literally falling apart. In 1502, during his fourth voyage to the Caribbean, Columbus survived a hurricane, lightning, water spouts, and coral reefs, only to find that two of his four ships had to be abandoned because of shipworm infestation. Magellan also lost one of his ships to these unseen wood-eaters.

But what are these little critters that can cause us so much grief? The shipworm is not a worm at all, but rather a highly specialized mollusk, or clam. Its shell is greatly reduced in size and is modified into a rasp for grinding the wood that provides the cellulose for its unique diet. The shipworm, which only lives in salt water, invades new wood when it is in its microscopic larval stage. In this stage it is free-swimming, and its initial entrance hole into wood is no bigger than a pinhole, making it hard to detect. Once inside edible wood, the shipworm begins eating and growing, and some species, such as those in the Caribbean, can attain a length of over 3 feet. In our waters, however, the shipworm seldom attains a length of over a foot-and-a-half long. Since the shipworm remains in the interior of the wood structure, its worm-like body is protected from predators. The first hint of problems comes after the interior of the wood is nearly completely devoured and the outside wooden shell of the piling, bulkhead, or boat-planking disintegrates. This is the same attack plan as the land-based termite, which also remains undetected inside the wood, so it's not surprising that the shipworm has been called "the termite of the sea."

Another destroyer of wood is the gribble (*Limnoria*). This tiny salt water isopod most often attacks the surface of wood.

Throughout our waters wooden bulkheads at marinas, public docks, and private homes are now failing at a remarkable rate. Most wood bulkheads that have been destroyed by shipworms are now being replaced with vinyl bulkheading material. Although more expensive than either creosoted or chemically-treated wood, vinyl provides the dual advantages of an extended life—probably about fifty years—and, since it isn't treated with poisonous chemicals, it has a minimal impact on the immediate aquatic environment.

There's really no way to eliminate these wood-eaters from our waters, and we really don't want to, since our relationship with these critters isn't all bad. These same animals that can give us so much grief are also responsible for eliminating trees and branches that are washed into our navigable waterways during storms. They are nature's way of providing a natural clean-up system.

As we continue on, we head for the destination of most transients, the marinas on the south, under the hills of the highlands, or an anchorage such as Horseshoe Cove, inside of Sandy Hook. From the Verrazano Bridge it's a straight-line trip across the bay to these locations. As we head south from the Narrows, we pass the tiny Hoffman and Swinburne islands to the west of the marked channel. The New Jersey/New York state line runs roughly east and west down the center of the bay, midway between the New Jersey Highlands and the Narrows, so we are now returning to New Jersey waters.

The 80-square-mile bay supports and amazing variety of fish, shellfish, and crustaceans, in fact, lobster traps are now being used in the bay and are yielding a reasonable catch. The bottom of the bay is covered with clams, more than any other region of New Jersey, but they are off-limits for recreational harvesting. A few years ago a program was set up so that commercially harvested bay clams, under strict supervision by the state, could be transported to Lacey Township in Ocean County, where a "clam relay station" has been set up in Barnegat Bay. The clams are left in the clean waters of the bay for up to sixty days, depending on the time of year. There they purge themselves of any toxins and could then be sold commercially.

In 1991 the Port Authority awarded Atlantic Highlands a $1.3 million grant to build a clam depuration plant—a plant that uses oxygen, cold, pure water, and ultraviolet light to kill harmful bacteria—as an alternative to the clam relay station.

During World War I and World War II, Sandy Hook served as an artillery base, ostensibly used as an area from which to guard the entrance to New York Harbor. Sandy Hook's armament included Nike missiles before its military career came to an end in 1975. At its northern tip, the old ammunition bunkers

The Sandy Hook Lighthouse as seen from Sandy Hook Bay

and gun emplacements of Fort Hancock and the historic Sandy Hook Lighthouse share space with a Coast Guard base. The majority of land on Sandy Hook is now under the jurisdiction of the National Park Service.

The popular anchorage of Horseshoe Cove is about 2 miles down from the tip of Sandy Hook on the bay side. The approach to Horseshoe Cove from the north takes us past yellow-brick buildings that were once used as officers' quarters. Just beyond is the rubble of concrete bunkers at water's edge, remnants of World War II. These bunkers are just to the north of Horseshoe Cove and serve as a good landmark. Fish nets sometimes extend into the bay, well out from shore. Make the approach outside of these nets. There is a sandspit extending south that encloses the northwest side of the cove and stretches under water for a considerable distance. Portions of it are awash at low tide. The southern end of this underwater bar is marked by a white can buoy with a red diamond. Entering the cove south of this buoy is the rule. The other similar white buoys at the southern end of the anchorage are no-wake markers. On shore, near the footbridge at the north end of the anchorage, are drums for garbage and recyclables. Horseshoe Cove is a popular anchorage, and on summer weekends can be crowded. It's a good idea to check the weather report before anchoring; the cove offers no protection from west winds, which can make for an uncomfortable overnight stay.

The World War II bunker ruins just north of Horseshoe Cove

There are few places in the northeast that are more of a nautical cross-roads than Sandy Hook Bay. To the north we see the Narrows, spanned by the Verrazano Bridge, with the skyscrapers of Manhattan beyond. A trip north through the Narrows, New York Harbor, and the East River, brings us to Long Island Sound and New England waters. To the west is Raritan Bay, leading to the Raritan River or to the protected waterways around the west side of Staten Island. Eastward, to the south of Long Island, is the offshore passage to New England, and thirty miles to the south, down along the New Jersey coast, is Manasquan Inlet and the entrance to the Intracoastal Waterway (the ICW), which provides a protected passage all along the east coast to the Mexican border.

Along the south shore of Sandy Hook Bay are several marinas. The Atlantic Highlands Municipal Marina is the largest. It is nestled at the foot of the hill that is the highest point of land on the east coast between New York and Florida—hence the name "The Highlands." On top of this hill is the famous Twin Lights Lighthouse, which is open to the public but is no longer operational. The Highlands was the first view of the new world for millions of immigrants who came by ship to this country over the past 350 years. The Atlantic Highlands Municipal Marina usually has transient slips available, which can accommodate the largest of craft—up to 170 feet—however on summer weekends a call ahead for a reservation would be prudent. This is a full-service marina which includes a restaurant, showers, and tennis courts. Other amenities, such as an ATM, propane, Laundromat, repair services, movie house, bank, post office, supermarket, convenience store, restaurants, and liquor store are in town within walking distance. At the marina is a high-speed ferry service to downtown Manhattan (less than an hour), as well as charter and party boats, and a dinner-cruise boat. Sunday summer concerts are held at the nearby gazebo, and a short distance away is Sandy Hook National Park, with ocean and bay beaches. If a slip is not available a transient can drop the hook within the eastern end of the three-quarter-mile-long stone breakwater, if there is room. When anchoring, be sure to stay out of the approach channel to the marina and allow for the tide.

The hill of the Highlands has been important to navigation since the first explorers used it as the landmark to locate the entrance to New York Harbor. Frequently the old sailing ships would stop at the foot of the Highlands, in Sandy Hook Bay, to replenish their water supply from the "Spout," a clear, cool spring that still flows today. The 1609 log from Henry Hudson's *Half Moon* shows that he dropped anchor there and sent his men ashore for water. Captain Kidd put into New Jersey often—to bury treasure, say the romantics. More probably his stops at the Highlands were to fill his water casks before a priva-

Aerial view of the Atlantic Highlands Municipal Marina (photo courtesy of Keith Hamilton, Studio-9, Waretown)

teering foray. The spring was first used by the Lenape Indians (whose name appropriately means "first people"), and then by the early European settlers, but the spring's water flow has diminished greatly since those days. It is now locally known as "Henry Hudson's Spring," and a bronze plaque nearby commemorates its history.

After a quiet night at an anchorage or in a marina, it's now time to explore Sandy Hook Bay, Raritan Bay, and their tributaries. Sandy Hook, on the eastern end of this large body of water, is part of the National Gateway recreation Area, with facilities including ocean and bay swimming beaches, surf fishing, nature trails, and picnic areas. At the Spermaceti Cove Visitor's Center near the entrance to the Sandy Hook Recreation Area are maps and brochures. The Sandy Hook Lighthouse, an 88-foot octagonal tower, is the oldest working lighthouse in the country. Not only is it still navigational, but it is now a historical monument. It is one of the two lighthouses along the New Jersey coast that are still active. The other is the Cape May lighthouse.

In 1762, when Sandy Hook's lighthouse was built, it was just 500 feet from the tip of the hook, the logical location from which to guide boats through the deep-water channel that leads into Sandy Hook Bay. Since then Sandy Hook has been extending north, so much so that the lighthouse now stands more

Henry Hudson's spring

than a mile and a half from the hook's northern tip. Such is our ever-changing coastline. At various times in history, Sandy Hook has been either a peninsula or an island, as Sandy Hook Inlet, at the base of the hook has opened and closed.

At the southeastern corner of Sandy Hook Bay is a waterway that leads to the "twin rivers," the Navesink and the Shrewsbury (chart 2.1). This area was the setting for James Fenimore Cooper's novel *The Water Witch,* the name of a ghost ship that sailed Sandy Hook Bay's waters in the early 1700s. The entrance to the Shrewsbury River is via a buoyed channel that passes through a bascule bridge that connects the Highlands with the ocean beaches. Tides in this waterway can be swift, and auxiliaries should allow for delayed bridge openings and congested boat traffic. Adjacent to the bascule bridge is Bahr's Restaurant and Marina, one of the oldest on the New Jersey shore.

Just past the bridge, the Navesink River, which is more of a tidal estuary than a true river, branches off to the west, and has a navigable channel for 6 miles up to Red Bank. In Red Bank only small craft will be able to go farther up the river, beyond the fixed Route 35 highway bridge (with an 8-foot clearance) near the head of navigation. The Navesink was originally called the North Shrewsbury, confirming their relationship as twin rivers. The channel entering the Navesink cuts between shoals, and the channel depth at low tide

The waterway and bascule bridge leading to the Navesink and Shrewsbury rivers

has been reported to be 2.5 feet in spots, so straying outside the marked channel can easily create a delay until the next tide change. Once past the bascule bridge and the shoals, facilities for transients are on the south shore, and anchorages with good holding can be found under the high bluffs in this residential environment, which is one of the most beautiful estuaries along our coastline. At the head of navigation, about five and a half miles up from the entrance, is the town of Red Bank, with marinas and restaurants at water's edge, and where the Riverview Medical Center are located.

Perhaps the most famous of the restaurants along the Navesink in Red Bank is the Molly Pitcher Inn and Marina, located near the Route 35 bridge. The inn, a landmark since 1928, is easily recognizable, designed to resemble Philadelphia's Independence Hall. It is named, of course, for the heroine of the battle of Monmouth during the Revolution. The seventy-slip marina at the foot of the hill below the inn has sixteen docks for transients, can accommodate large vessels, and is a short walk from the stores in town. On weekends there is a two-night-minimum stay at the marina.

The waters of the Navesink have been steadily improving during the last few years. This is due to a joint program that was implemented by federal, state, and local agencies. The water quality is so good that, for the first time in nearly thirty years, the Department of Environmental Protection has recommended the opening of a large area of river bottom (east of McClees Creek) for the direct harvest of soft clams during the winter season.

There is a Baykeeper Oyster Restoration program underway in these waters, under the auspices of the American Littoral Society and the New York/New Jersey Baykeeper. During the summer months hundreds of volunteers plant between 50,000 and 100,000 oysters on the Navesink oyster reef in Red Bank and on the reef in Keyport Harbor. These oysters are raised in cages at private docks by volunteers and are transplanted into Navesink's waters when they are about a year old. Over time the restored oyster beds will filter and help purify the water, while creating more young oysters,

The Shrewsbury and Navesink Rivers have been declared a "No Discharge Zone," which means that the only acceptable type of on-board head is one that uses a holding tank.

If one follows the waterway from Sandy Hook Bay, and past the entrance to the Navesink, and under the bridge that joins Rumson Neck and Sea Bright (with a 15-foot closed clearance), one will enter into the bay portion of the Shrewsbury River.

This part of the Shrewsbury is one of the prettiest of any of New Jersey's inland tidewaters and always reminds me of a miniature Chesapeake Bay. Not only is the similarity of the natural features striking (if one looks at the chart), but the ambiance is the same. The banks of the bay are serrated with coves, brooks, streams, and miniestuaries; and along the banks are private docks, yacht clubs, marinas, and shoreside restaurants, along with homes that range in size from mansions to condominiums. Most of the Shrewsbury is shallow, but the channels off the main waterway are well marked, and an exploration of the many little side streams and coves by dinghy can prove an enchanting sojourn.

As we cruise through these waters, many maritime anecdotes from the past come to mind. It was just over a century ago, in 1894, that Simon Lake, a native of Toms River, made one of the world's first submarines. The *Argonaut Junior* was fourteen feet long, made of yellow pine, and designed so that when submerged she could travel along the bottom of the river or bay on its three wheels, powered by a hand crank. A compressed-air soda-fountain tank provided the pressurization. The submarine was launched at Atlantic Highlands, and Simon Lake Drive now marks the launching spot. From there it was paddled to the Shrewsbury River, where the crew made their first underwater run, traveling along the bottom of the Shrewsbury at a moderate walking gait.

Lake's later designs were sold to the U. S. Navy, as well as to several European nations, and included his invention of the periscope and torpedo

Chart 2.1 Navesink and Shrewsbury Rivers (reproduced from NOAA's Chart #12324)

The Navesink River

The Shrewsbury River

tubes. These contracts grossed millions, but Lake was a poor businessman and died in poverty in 1945.

We now leave these historic river estuaries and head back to Sandy Hook Bay, where we continue our exploration of the shoreline, heading west from the hook toward the separately named but indistinguishable waters of Raritan Bay.

There are many marinas along these shores. One of them, the Leonardo State Marina is one of four in New Jersey that is owned by the state. The others are the Forked River State Marina in Lacey Township, off Barnegat Bay; the Senator Frank S. Farley State Marina in Atlantic City; and the Fortescue State Marina in Cumberland County on the north shore of Delaware Bay.

Note that a security zone exists around the 2-mile-long government pier that extends out into the bay just west of the Leonardo State Marina—stay well away. This pier is used for loading and unloading munitions, as would be indicated by its name, the Earl Ammunition Pier. In May of 1950 an ammunition explosion occurred on the docks, killing thirty-one dock workers, shattering doors and windows for miles around, and showering debris and soot over a huge area. The explosion was heard as far away as Pennsylvania.

To the west of the Earl Ammunition Pier, pound nets can be encountered along shore, making nighttime travel difficult or even hazardous. We've seen

The government pier in Sandy Hook Bay

these nets off Port Monmouth, Keansburg, and along the shore to the east of Cheesequake Creek. Although they are required to be lighted, the dim lights are often difficult to separate from the lights on shore. Occasionally small strobe lights mark the nets, and some have radar reflectors on the poles.

All along the southern shore of Raritan Bay there are municipal and county beaches. Water quality is checked regularly, and in recent years there have been few closings.

Compton Creek and Belford Harbor, just west of the government pier, are devoted to commercial fishing boats, seiners, draggers, lobsterers, and the like. In Belford Harbor the fishing captains established the Belford Seafood Cooperative in 1956, which is housed in a large building beside the water. Fish are sold both wholesale and retail. The harbor is reminiscent of a New England fishing village, but currently it is unlikely that a recreational boat would find a berth there. Nevertheless, a cruise through the harbor is a fascinating diversion, as the traveler briefly visits the world of the commercial ocean fishing industry. To enter, follow the entrance buoys in off the bay. At the last buoy, just before shore, a ninety degree left turn takes one south of the high stone breakwater and into the harbor.

About a mile northwest of Compton Creek is Pews Creek, where the channel has about 6 feet of water going to the marinas. Inside the creek, on its east

Belford Harbor

shore, is a large marina and park operated by the Monmouth County Park Commission, and just beyond is a private marina. Thorns Creek at Keansburg also has some limited facilities for small- to medium-sized craft.

Matawan Creek at Keyport is easily entered through its buoyed entrance channel. The Keyport Yacht Club and a marina are just to the east of the entrance to the creek, and the entrance channel continues past the moored sailboats on both east and west sides. These moored boats, easily seen with the aid of field glasses from the bay, provide a good landmark for Matawan Creek's entrance channel. Once inside, the fishing fleet is immediately to port, followed by the town dock, which is suitable for use by ship's tender. There are marinas on both sides of the channel before the first bridge (that has a 6-foot clearance) as well as farther up the waterway, beyond this bridge and the following 12-foot fixed bridge. Stores, restaurants, and a Ferry Museum are within walking distance of the marinas.

Farther west along the south shore of Raritan Bay is Cheesequake Creek. The entrance is between stone breakwaters with skeletal towers on their outer ends. The easterly breakwater is submerged at high tide and will not show up on radar, so a short cut will put you on the rocks. On weekends there are many boats anchored off the breaches in this area, where the hard sand

The distinctive headlands at Keyport Harbor can be easily identified through the haze

The entrance to Cheesequake Creek off Raritan Bay

Cheesequake Creek, with the Garden State Parkway Bridge in the background

bottom provides good holding. The Route 35 bascule bridge (with closed clearance of 25 feet) is just inside the entrance to the creek. There is a convenient marina on Stumps Creek, which branches off Cheesequake Creek to the east, beyond the bascule bridge but ahead of the railroad bridge. The railroad bridge (with a closed clearance of 3 feet) is usually in the open position unless a train is expected. Locally, the Cheesequake is called Morgan's Creek so, when calling the railroad bridge tender, call for the Morgan railroad bridge. Further up Cheesequake Creek, beyond the railroad bridge, there are several large marinas that one passes before reaching the Garden State Parkway's 8-foot fixed bridges. These marinas are very popular with recreational boaters, particularly those who own sailboats, in spite of some typical bridge-opening problems. The Cheesequake was once the home of the famous Luhr Boatyard, where Henry Luhr's beautiful wooden boats were built for many years, prior to the popularity of fiberglass.

Two and a half miles due north from Cheesequake Creek, across this western corner of Raritan Bay, is the entrance to the Arthur Kill, which separates New Jersey and Staten Island. (Arthur Kill was described in chapter 1.) At one time this western end of Raritan Bay contained one of the best oyster grounds on the east coast, until pollution and sediment accumulation destroyed it.

The entrance to Arthur Kill as seen from Raritan Bay

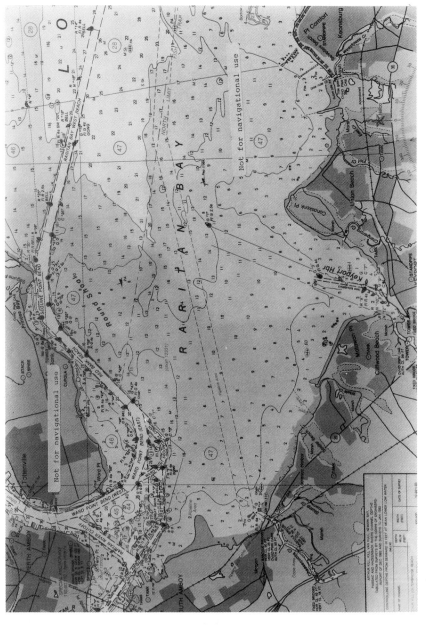

Chart 2.2 Western end of Raritan Bay (reproduced from NOAA's Chart #12327)

To the west is the entrance to the Raritan River, with South Amboy on its south bank and Perth Amboy on its north bank (chart 2.2). The name "Amboy" derives from the original 1651 land deed (the land was deeded from the Lenape Indians), when the area was called "Empoyle." This became "Ampoyle," and finally "Amboy."

The Raritan River flows 11 miles through meadowlands that have been virtually untouched by industry or development, finally reaching the head of navigation at New Brunswick, the home of Rutgers University.

The Raritan is the longest river within New Jersey, approximately 100 miles in length from the headwaters of the south branch to Raritan Bay. The name Raritan can be traced to the Naraticong Indian tribe of the Raritang nation, who lived along the river and used the river as their primary mode of travel.

Long before the most primitive of roads had been established, Native Americans had beaten a trail across the state that was later used to carry furs for trade in the New York City area. The trail was forged from the most southerly of the Delaware River's fording areas, the rapids at Trenton, to the most easterly of the fording areas on the Raritan near the present city of New Brunswick, and then on to New York. Old deeds referred to it as the Indian Path, and it finally became the dividing line between Somerset and Middlesex counties.

In later years the trail became an important stagecoach thoroughfare; then a railroad right-of-way, and finally an automobile artery, the New Jersey Turnpike, one of the busiest highways in the world.

During the early years of colonization, captains brought their sailing ships up the Raritan River to fill their water casks before long voyages because the water was so sweet and pure. Eventually, an increase in population and a gross disregard for the basic tenets of ecology and sanitation created impurities in Raritan's waters, making it unusable for fish, fowl, or humans. It wasn't until the mid-1920s that the government started to acknowledge the problem, and only in recent years, under pressure from environmental groups, have concrete steps been taken to improve the quality of the river's water.

At the entrance to the Raritan River is a railroad bridge, which is normally open, except when commuter trains are approaching.

Beyond the Garden State Parkway bridge, there are no bridges for 7 miles until we reach the fixed bridge of the New Jersey Turnpike, just before entering New Brunswick and Highland Park. Since there is virtually no industry along this segment of the river, commercial traffic is almost nonexistent and the trip is a pleasant winding tour through the wetlands. On approaching the

The entrance to the Raritan River as seen from Raritan Bay

New Brunswick area, the river banks become higher and are populated with summer cabins and year-round homes.

Farther up the Raritan, just west of the New Jersey Turnpike Bridge, we approach New Brunswick on the south bank and Highland Park on the north bank. This is where the river ceases to be navigable, but it wasn't always so. At one time, it was the starting point of the Delaware and Raritan Canal, an important commercial link between the port of New York and the Delaware River near Trenton and Philadelphia.

The idea of a canal connecting the Raritan and Delaware rivers across the narrow, 35-mile wide, waist of New Jersey had been discussed since the earliest colonial times. The advantages were obvious. The industrial ports of New York City and northern New Jersey could be connected with those of Philadelphia, Camden, and Trenton, eliminating the torturous trip of more than 260 miles out into the Atlantic, through Delaware Bay, and up the Delaware River. Since the Raritan flowed due west at this point, it was a natural location for the connecting link. Digging was finally begun in 1804 and completed in 1829. Although, as the crow flies, it is only about 25 miles from New Brunswick to the Delaware River, due to the topography the canal trip was 44 miles long, ending in Bordentown, just south of Trenton.

As soon as the canal opened the traffic was heavy, rivaling the tonnage and revenue of the Erie Canal, but the canals in the northeast were already

Approaching New Brunswick on the Raritan River

The Delaware and Raritan Canal Park in New Brunswick

A cruise up South River

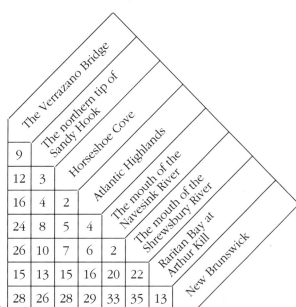

Table 2

Distances Between Locations

(in statute miles to the nearest mile)

The Verrazano Bridge	The northern tip of Sandy Hook	Horseshoe Cove	Atlantic Highlands	The mouth of the Navesink River	The mouth of the Shrewsbury River	Raritan Bay at Arthur Kill	New Brunswick
9							
12	3						
16	4	2					
24	8	5	4				
26	10	7	6	2			
15	13	15	16	20	22		
28	26	28	29	33	35	13	

being threatened by the railroads. In the same decade that the Delaware and Raritan Canal began hauling freight and passengers, the railroads increased their miles of track from a mere 23 miles in 1830 to more than 2,800 miles by 1840. It wasn't long before the railroads were moving more freight at a higher speed, and canals fell into disuse. The Delaware and Raritan Canal was finally closed and many sections were filled in. We're fortunate that long sections of the canal have been preserved and are now part of county and state park systems, conserving this historical waterway for future generations. The parks use the canal and the original towpath along its banks for walking, biking, jogging, horseback riding, fishing, picnicking, and boating.

Another fascinating cruise in this region is South River. South River joins the Raritan River on the south side, a few miles from its mouth. A cruise heading south up the South River is surprising. In one of the most congested parts of the United States, we feel as if we were in the middle of nowhere. Wetlands border the river and few signs of human life can be seen till, finally, we approach the head of navigation at the quaint town of South River.

*O*ur cruise throughout the Raritan Bay region now comes to a close as we prepare for the offshore passage from Sandy Hook, heading south. Have a good night's sleep in preparation for the ocean voyage tomorrow.

Chapter Three

Sandy Hook to Manasquan Inlet and the Intracoastal Waterway to Toms River

From our protected anchorage in Raritan Bay or in Sandy Hook Bay, we'll now take the ocean leg of our trip south.

The east coast's Intracoastal Waterway system (the "ICW") is made up of bays, sounds, estuaries, and rivers, protected from the ocean by barrier islands and joined together in many places with man-made cuts, or canals. Although the ICW allows the small boat owner to travel in relatively benign waters all the way from New York to the Mexican border, one section of that project was never completed; that is the section between the Manasquan River and Sandy Hook. It is the only place on the ICW where the skipper of a small craft is obligated to go out into the ocean. So after checking a NOAA weather channel (WX-1 for New York City, WX-5 for Holmdel (just northwest of Manasquan Inlet), and WX-2 for Atlantic City) as well as checking the weather visually, and with the boat prepared for an offshore trip, we head out.

Since we do most of our cruising in our two-masted schooner *Delphinus*, we are limited to a hull speed of about 7 knots maximum, so we always start our ocean trip south from the bay at first light. The typical wind pattern along the New Jersey coast and intracoastal waters is diurnal, that is, it has a daily recurring pattern: Calm in the morning; then, about 11 a.m., the sea breeze begins to pick up as the land warms; wind speeds off the ocean increase till about 4 p.m., they die down again by sunset. The afternoon wind can become very strong, considerably stronger than the forecasted speed, and along with the summertime possibility of afternoon thunderstorms, this can make inlet entrances less than pleasant—so an early start in the morning is recommended.

Marginal weather should be carefully considered. When deciding whether or not to wait, take into account both the skipper's and the crews' experience and ability, as well as the seaworthiness of the boat.

The Atlantic coastline of New Jersey stretches 127 miles south from Sandy Hook. The shoreline is relatively straight, with fairly constant slope waters and a sandy bottom. Most of the coastline consists of a series of barrier islands, broken intermittently by inlets, varying from excellent to unusable. These inlets continue to form, change, or close, as storms pound vengeful waves against the barrier islands and as high seas, whipped up by nor'easters and hurricanes, recarve the coastline.

Visual navigation along the coast in clear weather from a couple of miles offshore presents no special problems. Water towers display each town name, and the hill at the Highlands, the Ferris wheel at Seaside, Barnegat Lighthouse, the casinos and high rises at Atlantic City, and the Lighthouse at Cape May, can be seen from great distances.

As we check our charts we discover the astonishing fact that from this point, the trip by boat to Trenton, New Jersey is longer than a boat trip to Boston, Massachusetts. This is a dramatic testimony to the extent of New Jersey's navigable waters.

Taking Sandy Hook Channel around the tip of Sandy Hook out into the ocean, we usually see some small boats close to shore in False Hook Channel (chart 3.1). This is a "local Knowledge" route and best left to the locals. Near the tip of the hook, a condition known as the "Sandy Hook rip" exists when wind and tide are in opposition. This usually occurs just to the northeast of False Hook Channel and can make things a trifle nasty; unexpected breakers can pop up and ruin the whole day. Even though you might want to examine the fauna on Sandy Hook's nude beach, from a safety standpoint it's better to take Sandy Hook Channel out about 2 miles, then head south and closer to shore again, if desired. At this point our trolling lure is dropped off the stern, usually guaranteeing one or more bluefish to restock the larder before returning to inland waters.

We frequently make the trip just a few hundred yards offshore, sightseeing our way south. Once, just south of the hook, a sudden fog engulfed us and visibility decreased to just a boat length. Advection fogs such as this are common from early spring through June and occur whenever warm, humid air overruns the, as yet, cold ocean. We had no Loran or GPS on board (this was before those navigational aids were available to recreational boats) but rather than return inside the Sandy Hook we used our compass, depth-sounder, and an old RDF (Radio Direction Finder), slowly continuing our way through the sodden gray mist and following the 30-foot contour (about a mile offshore and well inside the shipping lanes) all the way down to Barnegat Inlet. We followed a relatively straight line, making for an uneventful trip, and we were happy to discover the entrance buoys to Barnegat Inlet and return to inland waters.

South of Sandy Hook we pass the Highlands. A lighthouse has been in operation on top of the hill here since 1762. The original lighthouse was built by a consortium of New York City merchants to ensure safe arrival of their ships. The twin towers of the present lighthouse were rebuilt in 1862 and were dedicated by President Lincoln. Standing at a total height of merely 246 feet, they are, to this day, located on the highest ground on the Atlantic coast between New York and Key West. The twin lights of the Highlands were the first indication of an arrival to the New World seen by tens of thousands of immigrants approaching this coastline during the evening hours.

If you look closely, you will see that the twin towers are not identical twins. The square-shaped south tower has sixty-five steps to its top, while the octagonally-shaped north tower has sixty-four. When they were operational, the lights shone through 7-foot Fresnel lenses, providing the most powerful beacons in the country until they were decommissioned in 1949. The towers are listed on the current charts as abandoned.

Traveling south from the Highlands, the next major ocean-side resort is

The ocean beach at Sandy Hook and the Sandy Hook Lighthouse

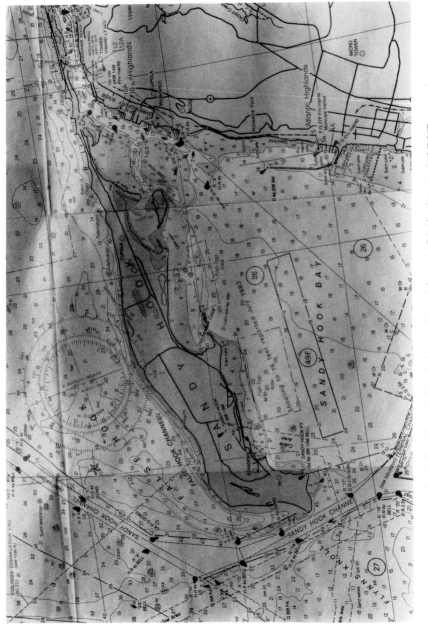

Chart 3.1 Sandy Hook (reproduced from NOAA's Chart #12327)

The Highlands and Twin Lights

Long Branch. It was once the unofficial summer resort of U.S. presidents, and it was also the place James Garfield went to die after being mortally wounded by an assassin's bullet. The carnival games and attractions along the boardwalk were one of Long Branch's big tourist attractions until they were destroyed by fire in June 1987. From here, on a clear day, we will be able to see the pier at Asbury Park, jutting out into the ocean.

As one ocean-side resort follows another, we head south along the coastline and don't even need our Loran, GPS, or radar, since checking off the route on the chart via water towers and prominent buildings is more fun. Clear, calm days, however, are the most practical time to hone navigational skills, when electronic read outs and dead reckoning can be compared to visual observations. Aside from the enjoyment and practice, having an up-to-date chart on board and knowing how to use it is the cheapest boat insurance on the market.

Fifteen miles south from the tip of Sandy Hook, we pass the Convention Hall Pier at Asbury Park. Each time we sail past I remember the September day in 1934 when my family gathered on the beach to see the still-burning hull of the cruise ship *Morro Castle*. It lay aground, broadside to the beach, just beyond the surf line, its stern less than 100 yards from Asbury Park pier, and its bow close to the stone jetty. Some of the bodies of the 134 who perished had already begun to wash ashore at New Jersey's resort beaches, and it took weeks before the ship was finally towed free and eventually broken up for scrap.

In September of 1994, just over sixty years after the disaster, survivors of the *Morro Castle* disaster met at the Sea Girt Lighthouse in what may have been their last reunion. Several books and articles about the strange events that led to the ship's demise, based on recently-released government documents that were obtained through the Freedom of Information Act, are now available and tell a bizarre story.

Seventeen miles below Sandy Hook and about 2 miles below Asbury Park is the Shark River inlet, the only small-craft harbor between Sandy Hook and Manasquan Inlet (chart 3.2). It's a popular spot for fishing, partying, and charter-boat rides, and has small-craft facilities, but it is navigable inland less than a mile and is not connected to the New Jersey Intracoastal Waterway in any way. The main channel is crossed by several bridges; the first is the Route 35 bridge, which is just inside the inlet. The Route 35 bridge across the Shark River had been an irritation to boaters and motorists alike since it was opened in 1927. For years there had been talk of replacing it with a high fixed bridge, and now it has finally happened. The new bridge actually consists of two separate spans for north and south bound road traffic.

Five miles farther south we are approaching the granite jetties at Manasquan Inlet and the beginning of the New Jersey Intracoastal Waterway.

One of my pet peeves is the frequent mispronunciation of *intracoastal*. Often I hear otherwise knowledgeable people saying intercoastal. Intercoastal means between one coast and another. A trip from New York City to Le Havre, France would be an intercoastal trip. Intracoastal means "within a coastline." The waterway on the east coast, built within the coastline inside the barrier islands is the Intracoastal Waterway.

The outer tips of the Manasquan Inlet's breakwaters are designated as the start of New Jersey's Intracoastal Waterway, *Mile-0*, which ends at Cape May. The ICW is shown on paper and electronic charts as a magenta-colored solid line, and at 5-mile intervals it is crossed by another magenta line, which indicates the number of statute miles from Mile-0. At night, when one is reading a paper chart using a red chart light, the magenta lines look black, as intended. Frequently, in descriptions of places along this inland route, I will use these ICW mile designations as a simpler means of describing a location than latitude and longitude.

Manasquan Inlet is normally easy to use, except when tides and strong winds are in opposition. The jetties have lights on their outer ends, but the fog horn on the south jetty has been discontinued. The huge amount of charter,

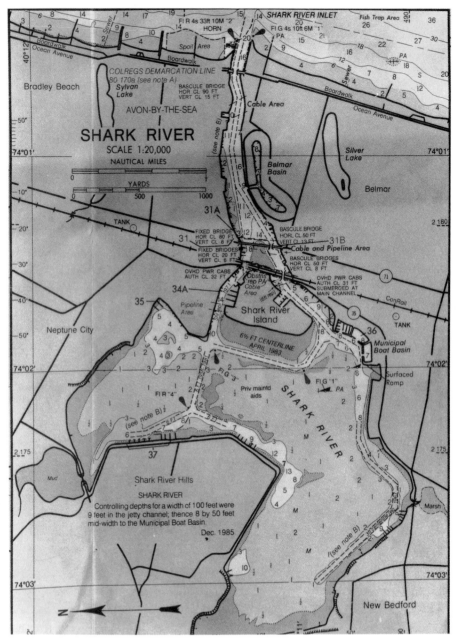

Chart 3.2 Shark River (reproduced from NOAA's Chart #12324)

Aerial view of Manasquan Inlet (photo courtesy of Keith Hamilton, Studio-9, Waretown)

commercial, and pleasure boat traffic using the inlet can make summer week-ends a bit hectic. New Jersey has more than 175,000 registered boats, and sometimes it seems as if they were all trying to use Manasquan Inlet. Once in-side the inlet, the towns of Brielle on the north and Point Pleasant on the south face each other across Manasquan River. (Manasquan is a name derived from the original Indian name "Manatahasquawhan." "Man-a-tah" meant island; "squaw," wife; and "han," river. Translated in its entirety, it means "River Island for Wives," and it was a place Indian men left their wives when they were away hunting and fishing.)

It is important to know that special regulations for the use of an on-board "head" exist in these waters. For most of New Jersey's waters the marine-head regulations that hold for all of United States waters are still in effect. That is, beyond 3 miles offshore a direct pump-out of untreated sewage is allowed (but discouraged). Within 3 miles of the shore, and for the intracoastal tidal waters, sewage that has been treated with a Coast Guard–approved on-board marine sanitation device (MSD), may be discharged. The only exception to the use of a MSD in intracoastal waters or up to 3 miles offshore is when an area has been designated as a "No Discharge Zone" (NDZ). In a No Discharge Zone no sewage may be discharged, even if it has been treated with a Coast Guard–approved on-board treatment system. For further information about on-board sewage disposal, consult "Marine Sanitation Devices" in the General Cruising Information section in the back of the book.

New Jersey's Intracoastal Waterway runs from Mile-0 at Manasquan Inlet down to Mile-115 at Cape May. The Navesink and Shrewsbury Rivers, Manasquan Inlet, Manasquan River, and the Point Pleasant Canal (covering ICW Mile-0 to Mile-4.5) were designated as a No Discharge Zone several years ago, and in June 2003 an additional 85 square miles of the intracoastal waters of New Jersey were also added to this NDZ. The waters in that new addition are termed the "Barnegat Bay Complex," and include the waters of Barnegat Bay and the separately-named waters of Manahawkin Bay and Little Egg Harbor. The tributaries into these bays are also included. The waters within this newly designated NDZ are to the west of the barrier islands of Island Beach and Long Beach Island.

This latest regulation expands the existing ICW No Discharge Zone so that it now goes from Manasquan Inlet south to ICW Mile-50.7. The demarcation line that is the southern end of this restricted zone extends west across the Intracoastal Waterway from the southern tip of Long Beach Island.

There are sixty-six pump-out stations and three pump-out boats in this area, and the total number of permanent boats in the Barnegat Bay Complex exceeds 30,000, which does not include transients. This translates to about 420 boats per pump-out station, which is within the EPA's guideline of 300–600 that allows an area to be designated a No Discharge Zone.

The U.S. Coast Guard is responsible for enforcement of this new regulation, but in a "Memorandum of Understanding," the New Jersey State Police, Marine Division, has been designated as the lead enforcement agency. These added duties will prove difficult, since the New Jersey Marine Police are already working under budget cuts and short-staffing.

Immediately inside the inlet at Point Pleasant on the south are the jointly owned, adjacent restaurants The Lobster Shanty and Wharfside. To reach them, follow the marked but uncharted channel toward the fishing-fleet docks. There are slips for transients and a dinghy dock behind the breakwater and in front of the Wharfside, but an overnight stay is not permitted.

There are small-craft facilities along both shores of the Manasquan River offering slips for transients, fuel, repairs, and haul-out services.

The largest of the Brielle marinas, on the north side of the river, is the Brielle Marine Basin, just to the west of the railroad bridge. It is a family-owned business that was started more than fifty years ago. Fuel, repairs, and a marine store are part of the marina, which has ten slips set aside for transients.

On the south shore of the river, just before the Point Pleasant Canal, one will find Clarks Landing Marina. It is a sports and fishing center that caters to family-oriented activities. The marina has a restaurant and lounge and a ship's store. There are many other fine marinas and yacht clubs along this busy two-mile stretch of waterway.

As we travel west up the Manasquan River, we go through a railroad bridge that is normally open but is very narrow, only 48 feet wide. This is immediately followed by the Route 35 bascule bridge, which has restricted opening hours. For all bridge information or to a request an opening, go to Channel-13. Be sure to use low power (1 watt) when transmitting, so that your call will not be received by other bridge operators in the area and cause confusion. Following the well-marked channel for another mile brings us to the entrance of the Point Pleasant Canal, a 2-mile long cut that joins the Manasquan River with the head of Barnegat Bay (chart 3.3).

Today's boaters take the extensive intracoastal waterway system for granted. But this massive project, that made the east coast a mecca for small boat enthusiasts, was only completed in relatively recent times.

It had always been a dream of small boat skippers on the East Coast to be able to travel from either New England, Long Island Sound, the Hudson River, or the Great Lakes, all the way to Florida, without ever having to cope with the open waters of the Atlantic Ocean. At the turn of the century the increase in commercial traffic on the water, as well as the heightening interest in pleasure boats, induced the state of New Jersey, and finally the federal government, to recognize the need for this inside waterway system between the mainland and the barrier islands. In 1908 New Jersey began dredging a channel inside of the barrier islands, north from Cape May. By 1915 the New Jersey section of the "Intracoastal Waterway" reached 111 miles, from Cape May to the northern end of Barnegat Bay. That same year the state obtained a right-of-way for a land cut that would extend this waterway from Bay Head, at the north end of Barnegat Bay, to the Manasquan River and Manasquan Inlet. This was originally called the Manasquan Canal and eventually came to be referred to as the Point Pleasant Canal.

From the very beginning the proposed Manasquan Canal was the subject of controversy. The residents at the north end of Barnegat Bay knew their freshwater paradise would be destroyed. It would mean the freshwater bass, bluegills, perch, and pike would cease to exist, and tides, salt water, and boat traffic would take over. In spite of this, the state kept digging until World War I forced suspension of the operation. Digging resumed after the war, and in

February 1926, with appropriate ceremonies, the Manasquan River and Barnegat Bay merged.

Then something unexpected happened. Within a few months after the opening of the Manasquan Canal, the unpredictable Atlantic closed Manasquan Inlet. Of course, the canal critics blamed it on the canal, suggesting that the new waterway diverted so much water that there wasn't enough flow to keep the inlet open. They may have been right. By August, the New Jersey National Guard had managed to open a narrow channel to the ocean, but it was a losing battle and the inlet closed completely by the year 1929. Local resident David Oxenford recalls: "I can't walk on water, but I can remember, as a child, walking across Manasquan Inlet."

Finally a joint county, state, and federal program was undertaken to cut through the dunes and beach and create a 400-foot wide inlet enclosed by stone jetties. The stone for these jetties came from an unlikely source. The New York subway system was being blasted out of the bedrock of Manhattan at that time, and the huge rocks were then barged down to Manasquan for the jetties. The new inlet was completed and opened in 1931.

Although the inlet worked as well as was expected, the tidal differences between Manasquan River at the north end of the 2-mile-long canal and Barnegat Bay at the south end sometimes exceeded 4 feet, creating exceptionally swift currents. Banks along the canal began to erode, and the footings of the bridges were undermined. Finally, in 1935, the newly formed Bureau of Commerce and Navigation undertook the bulkheading of both sides of the canal, a project whose initial phase was finally completed in 1937.

The canal proved its worth a few years later when, during World War-II, it allowed for oil barges and other commercial traffic to move inland, safe from the marauding U-boats that were hugging the New Jersey coast and the approaches to New York Harbor.

From the time of the Point Pleasant Canal's opening, the Route 88 bridge across the canal plagued boaters. More than once underpowered sailboats traveling with the tide had been carried down into the closed bridge and were damaged or demolished. Boats were often unable to make way against the opposing current. This problem occurred because during the height of tidal flow there was a perceptible difference in the water level on one side of the Route 88 bridge compared with the other. Only the most powerful of boats could push their way up hill, so to speak, to the other side.

There were so many problems with the Route 88 bridge that a new bridge was finally built, and in July 1986 it was opened to traffic. The old bridge was dismantled. At the same time, the stone shelf beneath the old bridge that had created a waterfall effect was removed. The horizontal clearance was nearly

Chart 3.3 Manasquan Inlet and Point Pleasant Canal (reproduced from NOAA's Chart #12324)

The Point Pleasant Canal

tripled, from the narrow 47 feet of the old bridge to 134 feet with the new one, putting an end to one of the Point Pleasant Canal's greatest threats.

Although used frequently by small boats of all types, the canal still retains some of its early characteristics. Most powerboats have no trouble negotiating the canal at any tidal stage. Even skippers of full-powered auxiliaries should find it no problem, though they can expect a slow trip against the tide. Operators of underpowered sailboats, small outboards, or any boat with inadequate

Aerial view of the Point Pleasant Canal (photos courtesy of Keith Hamilton, Studio-9, Waretown)

power should limit their transit to an hour or so either side of slack tide. The problem is determining when slack tide occurs. NOAA tidal current tables give the predicted time of slack water, which is, nominally, two to three hours after high or low tide in the ocean. However, times can vary greatly, depending on wind conditions (direction, strength, and duration). So, determining the time of slack water is chancy at best. One bridge operator remembers that once, during an extended blow, the tide in the canal didn't change direction for three days. Compounding the tide problems is the boat traffic during weekends and holidays, which can resemble rush hour on the streets of New York City.

There are two lift bridges that cross the canal. The northern bridge has a clearance of 31 feet when closed and 65 feet when open, and it responds to "Route 88 Bridge." The southern bridge has a 30-foot closed clearance and a 65-foot open clearance, and it answers to "Bridge Avenue Bridge." Both bridges open on demand, twenty-four hours a day, seven days a week. The bridgetenders can be reached on VHF CH-13 (use low power—1 watt). For those without VHF-FM, the standard one-long, one-short on the horn, is the alternative. Frequently, when it is obvious a sailboat is approaching and needs and opening, the bridges will open without being signaled.

Long before the Point Pleasant Canal was conceived, the lifestyle of the residents at each end of the proposed waterway consisted of divergent patterns. These patterns remain in place today. On the north, the Manasquan River is host to a large commercial and recreational fishing fleet, which uses the nearby Manasquan Inlet as their access to the ocean. The water traffic here can be frenetic near the inlet on a weekend at the height of the season, as boats rush back and forth from the fishing grounds. To the south of the canal, private homes crowd the banks, and water traffic is more leisurely. The shoreline is interspersed with recreational marinas and the old boatbuilders, who made the north end of Barnegat Bay famous in the first few decades of the 1900s. Recently a number of these boatbuilders consolidated under single ownership. They will still build boats to custom, but they also offer the other marine services expected by transients, including repairs, marine stores, and swimming pools.

The Intracoastal Waterway provides an inland route all the way from New York City to Miami, with the exception of the 28 statute miles from Sandy Hook to the Manasquan Inlet. At one time, many boaters bypassed Manasquan Inlet and took the offshore route, due to the many years of bad press about the Point Pleasant Canal. Now, with the new Route 88 bridge, there's no reason that a small boat with a draft of 5 feet or less shouldn't make use of the inside passage. If one combines a realistic assessment of power capabilities with a consideration of the day of the week and reasonable boating skills, this inside land cut can provide an interesting and picturesque passage—one that's much more pleasant than a trip outside in marginal weather, slugging it out with the Atlantic.

As we exit the south end of the Point Pleasant Canal, we enter the shallow waters of New Jersey's inland bays. In these relatively shoal waters wandering out of the channel can mean a grounding; but the bottom is forgiving, and the greatest damage will be to one's ego.

Once on New Jersey's intracoastal waters, boats can travel in any weather, short of a hurricane. The bay's bottom is sand and/or mud, and the Intracoastal Waterway is well marked. Late in 1991, at a cost of nearly a third of a million dollars, all the buoys on the NJ-ICW were renumbered, many were eliminated, and some were changed to different types. The nine different numbering systems that were previously used for the New Jersey section of the Intracoastal Waterway were eliminated and replaced by a single system. Now, all NJ-ICW buoys between the Point Pleasant Canal on the north and Cape May on the south have been numbered in sequential order from north to south. This was a long-needed improvement, and in the process many buoy locations were eliminated, while other buoys were replaced with more permanent poles. Although distances between navigational aids is now greater, the new pole markers can be seen at greater distance and will remain in place year-round (except for lighting equipment, which operates on solar-charged batteries which may be removed during the winter months). One can recognize ICW aids to navigation because, unlike others, they have a small yellow reflective panel near the buoy number.

Not only have inshore buoys been changed, but buoys at inlet entrances, as well as those at the entrance to Delaware Bay, have been changed both in number and position. If there are old charts on board, the present aids to navigation will bear no relationship in either type, number, or location to those shown on those charts.

At the north end of Barnegat Bay is the appropriately-named town of Bay Head. By land it is the last stop on New Jersey Transit's North Jersey Coast railroad line, making it attractive to those coming from the New York City area. In the last century this area was famous as a boat-building center. One of these boat-builders that is still in existence is the Johnson Brothers Boat Works, now a boatyard and marina. There you'll find the New Jersey Museum of Boating, Inc., which celebrates the state's rich boating history by preserving and displaying boats, equipment, scale models, and artifacts of a bygone era.

The ocean trip from New York's Lower Bay, through the Manasquan Inlet and the Point Pleasant Canal, is over and it might be time to call it a day.

Facilities for transients are available at one of the marinas around Bay Head or Mantoloking. If anchoring out, sipping cocktails, and relaxing in the cockpit for the evening seems like a good idea, we can take a trip up the spring-fed Metedeconk River to the west. Imposing homes nestled among the pine trees, private docks, yacht clubs, and marinas line the shore of this protected estuary, the name of which derives from the Lenape "Mittig-Cong," a place of good timber. As with most of New Jersey's waters that are more secluded, this 3.5-mile-long navigable channel up the wide Metedeconk is well marked with New Jersey buoys that are not shown on the federal chart. Water depth in this estuary is enough for most craft, nearly from shore to shore.

The sixty-five-year-old bridge across the ICW at Mantoloking (ICW mile 6.3) has a closed clearance of only 14 feet and has restricted opening times. For years it has caused problems for boaters and motorists alike since all sailboats and a large percentage of powerboats required the bascule to be opened for a passage. As of this writing plans were on the drawing board to replace this old structure with a new bascule bridge that will have a 30-foot closed clearance. The width of the waterway through the new bridge will be increased from 30 feet to 80 feet. Nearly all powerboats will be able to pass through the new bridge without opening it, however most sailboats will still require an opening. It is expected that the new bridge will decrease the yearly

The old Mantoloking Bridge

number of openings from approximately 6,000 to about 2,000. The new bridge will be built adjacent to the old one and, when finished, a section of the old bridge on the mainland side will become a fishing pier.

If we're inclined to press on a little farther south, Kettle Creek and the south shore of Silver Bay, next to the Cattus Island County Park, are attractive alternative choices as anchorages. The Cattus Island anchorage is not recommended when strong winds are from the northeast.

In central New Jersey there is an area called the Pine Barrens, 1.3 million acres of scrub pine, cedar, holly, blueberries, and cranberries. It is the largest open space between Washington, D.C., and Boston. In 1983 the United Nations designated the New Jersey Pine Barrens as an "International Biosphere Reserve." Most of the Pine Barrens, about 1.1 million acres, is protected under federal and state statutes. Just below the sandy loam of the barrens is a huge aquifer brimming with more than 17 trillion gallons of potable water, enough to cover the entire state of New Jersey with water more than 10 feet deep. Although located in the high-population density of the northeast corridor, the waters of this aquifer are some of the cleanest in the world. This reservoir gives birth to hundreds of little brooks and streams (stained brown by tannins from the cedar trees and by iron from the soil), which wend their way leisurely into the Delaware River basin to the west or toward the tidewaters of the Atlantic shoreline to the east. Only a few fish species have adapted to these highly acidic waters. Many of these streams and creeks join in the coastal plain a few miles west of the northern end of Barnegat Bay. There, the confluence of waters becomes an estuary that continues to widen and mix with salt, until finally merging with the bay waters. This estuary is the river of Toms River, just to the west of New Jersey's Intracoastal Waterway (at ICW mile 14.5).

The mouth of Toms River is just south of the twin bridges that span the ICW and carry Route 37 highway traffic between the mainland and the barrier island. The Route 37 bridges are side by side, one fixed and the other bascule. The newer fixed bridge on the north, the J. Stanley Tunney Bridge, has a 60-foot clearance and is used for traffic heading west. The older bascule bridge on the south, the Thomas A. Mathis Bridge, has a closed clearance of 30 feet and is used for highway traffic heading east. The bascule bridge has restricted opening hours. For those whose boats need to open bridges frequently (usually sailboats), a compilation of all the opening hours for bridges on the East Coast is listed in *The United States Coast Pilot,* a government publication that features comprehensive, up-to-date, and easy-to-follow listings of lights, buoys, sound signals, day-beacons, RACONS, radio beacons, and other aids to navigation maintained by or under the authority of the U.S. Coast Guard. The publication includes illustrations of aids to navigation and a glossary of terminology pertaining to these aids. Separate volumes are printed for each geographical area and may be obtained from the superintendent of documents, U.S. Government Printing Office, or from dealers of government charts.

Passing through the Route-37 bascule bridge while heading south marks a milestone, especially for sailboats. Sailboats with mast heights of under 53 feet that use the offshore route between Atlantic City and Cape May will not have to open any more bridges until the end of the cruise at Trenton. If an extended cruise south on the ICW is undertaken—one well to the south of New Jersey's waters—then the next bridge to be opened on the ICW is located just before the Dismal Swamp Canal, south of Norfolk, Virginia.

After passing under the Route 37 bridges, a trip to the west up Toms River will yield a selection of marinas or off-the-channel anchorages in a pleasant, protected atmosphere.

The channel up Toms River to the head of navigation is well buoyed, although these buoys are not shown on the chart (chart 3.4). Don't short-cut the marked channel at Long Point on the north; there is a shoal extending out from shore. The high banks along the north side of the river are dotted with many picturesque homes, and the Toms River Yacht Club, which was founded in 1871, is one of the oldest yacht clubs in the United States.

The Route 37 bridges between Toms River and Seaside Heights

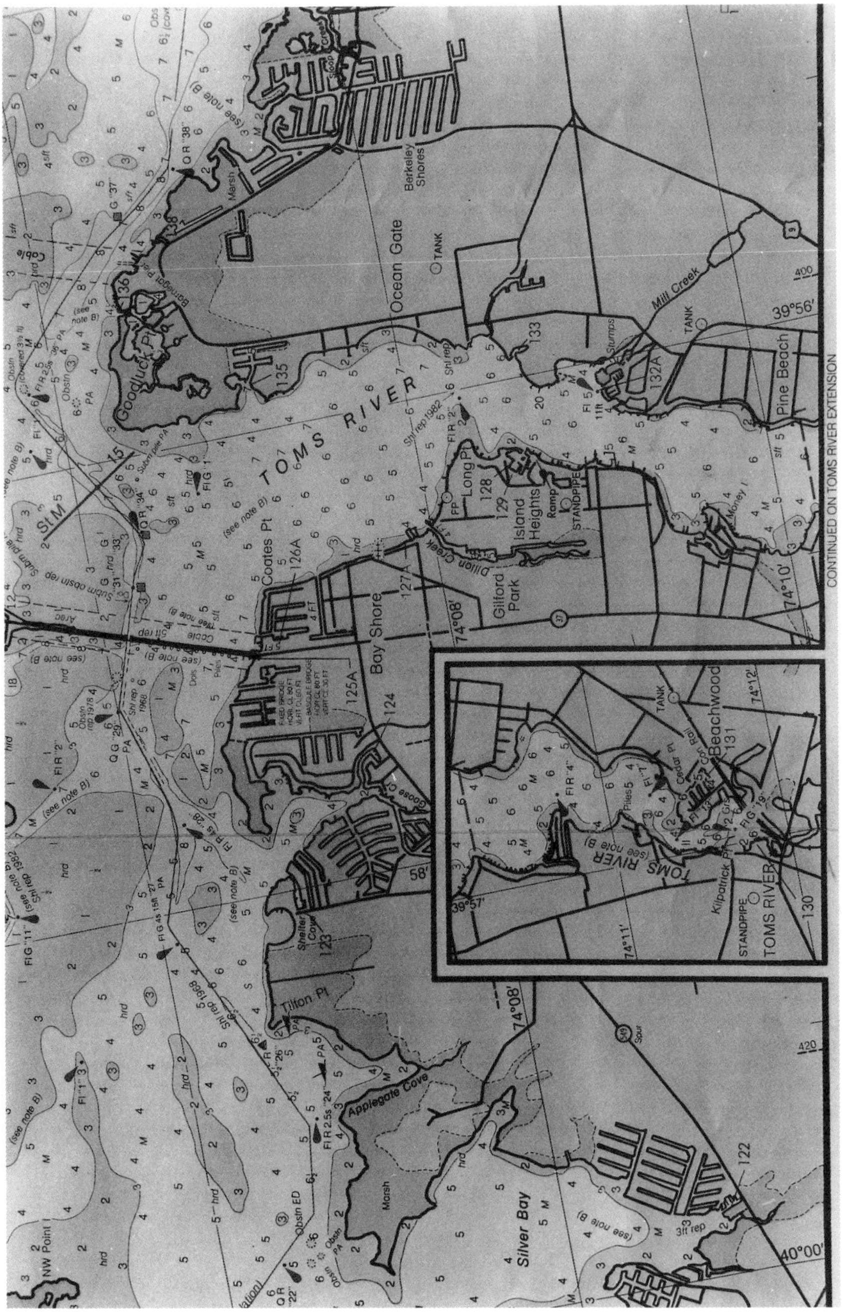

Chart 3.4 Toms River (reproduced from NOAA's Chart #12324)

Toms River

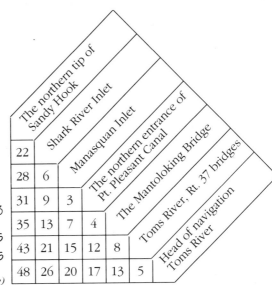

Table 3

Distances Between Locations

(in statute miles to the nearest mile)

	The northern tip of Sandy Hook	Shark River Inlet	Manasquan Inlet	The northern entrance of Pt. Pleasant Canal	The Mantoloking Bridge	Toms River, Rt. 37 bridges	Head of navigation Toms River
	22						
	28	6					
	31	9	3				
	35	13	7	4			
	43	21	15	12	8		
	48	26	20	17	13	5	

Toms River, the county seat of Ocean County, is a historic seaport that dates back to 1624. The origin of the town's name is obscured in legend and is much debated. One version has it that the town was named after Indian Tom, a Lenape Indian who made his home on its banks. Another, more likely, story is that the name came from Captain William Tom, who visited the area frequently during the 1600s. Toms River became an important seaport after 1740, when a storm cut through the barrier island directly across from the mouth of the river, creating a wide, deep inlet to the sea. This convenient inlet led Toms River to become a major port that was strategically important during the Revolutionary War. Because of Toms River's importance, the Tories, who were loyal to the King of England, burned the town to the ground in 1782. The local populace became so infuriated that the Loyalists were forced to leave the area until the end of the war.

In 1812, the inlet that had been created in the storm of 1740, the Cranberry Inlet, closed again during another storm, and despite persistent efforts that lasted until 1850, the inlet could never be kept open for any extended period. The land south of the Cranberry Inlet then became a peninsula again, attached to the mainland, though its name, Island Beach, remained. This marked Toms River's decline as an important ocean seaport, since ships were now obliged to use the more notorious Barnegat Inlet, more than 15 miles to the south.

The creation of new inlets across the barrier islands and the closing of old ones is not uncommon. An inlet across from the Metedeconk River, Herring

Inlet, and New Inlet, at the entrance to Island Beach, existed until the 1700s. Both of these inlets were closed by the storms of 1740, when Cranberry Inlet was created. More recently, the nor'easter of 1962 cut four new inlets across Long Beach Island. Three were rapidly closed. The fourth, a deep, broad inlet at Harvey Cedars, resisted the Army Corps of Engineers for some time, but it, too, was finally filled in.

As we travel up Toms River to the head of navigation, the waterway becomes narrower until we finally arrive in the center of town, about 4 miles from the mouth of the river. Many shops are within walking distance of the marinas, and the Lobster Shanty is a restaurant at the end of the river that has docks for small to medium-sized craft or ships' tenders.

Several small coves on both sides of the river offer protected anchorages off the main channel, under the high banks of the north shore, or protected from the prevailing winds along the south shore. Toms River, even for boats of displacement-hull speeds, is less than a days journey from Atlantic City, farther south on the NJ-ICW, or from New York City to the north.

Chapter Four

Barnegat Bay

About 80,000 years ago a global, or perhaps a cosmic, event transpired and our world began to turn cold. In the higher latitudes the snow never melted, accumulating for thousands of years and compressing into dense, thick sheets of ice. By 18,000 years ago, this northern glacier of ice, over 2 miles thick, had pushed its way south, grinding off the tops of mountains and shoving before it huge masses of stone and earth. At the same time the bottom of the glacier gouged out immense, deep valleys, such as the Great Lakes and the Finger Lakes. When a slight world warming trend occurred, the movement of this glacier stopped, with the southern boundary of the immense wall of ice extending east and west across northern New Jersey.

There was so much water tied up in the immense glaciers of this last ice age that the oceans' water levels dropped over 300 feet—enough to make the continental shelf dry land. What are now the bays and offshore waters of New Jersey was then a meadow with an elevation of 300 feet above sea-level, where Mastodons grazed on the grassy fields that extended over 100 miles to the east of where the shoreline is today. The ocean levels were so low that the shallow Bering Strait, between Asia and Alaska, became dry land, allowing nomadic Asian tribes to walk across and become the first Native Americans.

Finally, as with previous ice ages, this one also came to an end as the earth's temperature began to rise again, and by 14,000 years ago the glacier over New Jersey had retreated so that it only covered the Ramapo Mountains, in the northern part of the state. During this retreat immense amounts of water from the melting ice created the northeast rivers of today (which flowed south, away from the glacier). The melt began to fill up the oceans again and by 10,000 years ago, the sea level was close to what it is today.

In recent times the earth has been at its warmest since that last ice age. This global temperature increase could be the continuation of the warming cycle as we emerge from that ice age, but the especially warm temperatures of the last century or two also coincide with the beginning of the industrial revolution, as

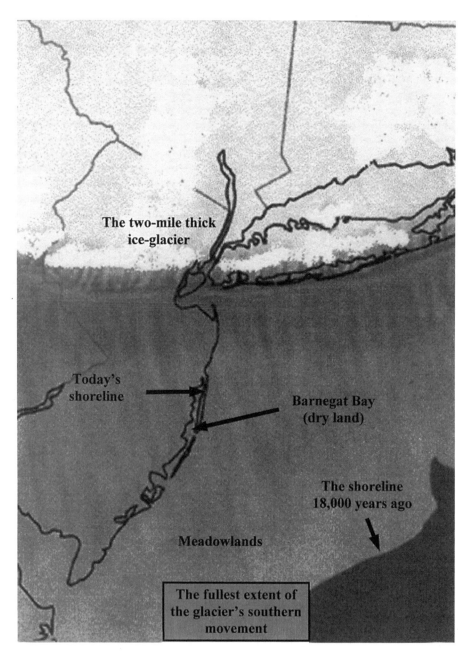

The two-mile thick
ice-glacier

Today's
shoreline

Barnegat Bay
(dry land)

The shoreline
18,000 years ago

Meadowlands

The fullest extent of
the glacier's southern
movement

*C*hart 4.1 The last ice age

greenhouse gases, created by man, are continually being pumped into the atmosphere. No one really knows whether man or nature claims the most responsibility for our current warming trend.

Over the last millennium, Native Americans migrated east from their early Bering Strait crossing, finally reaching the eastern seaboard about 4,000 years ago. Several tribes settled in the Barnegat Bay area, where they spent their summers harvesting fish, clams, oysters, and crabs. They also hunted the forest for the plentiful game and grew crops, using surprisingly sophisticated farming methods. Their stewardship of the land began to change, however, in the early 1600s with the encroachment of European settlers.

The date that the first white man came to these shores is lost in history. It's possible that the Vikings may have visited the Barnegat area about 1,000 years ago, and Giovanni da Verrazano may have visited here in 1524, but it wasn't until 1609 that Henry Hudson, in his awkward little Dutch craft, *The Half Moon,* first documented these shores. As he was heading north along the New Jersey coast, the ship's log records: "We came to a great lake of water . . . which was in length 10 leagues. The mouth of the lake has many shoals, and the sea breaks upon them. This is a very good land to fall in with and a pleasant land to see." The "lake" was Barnegat Bay, and the mouth of that lake, Barnegat Inlet, still has many shoals. In spite of hundreds of years of efforts to tame them, still "the sea breaks upon them."

When Europeans first began to settle along our shores the area was sparsely populated by Native Americans. The forests were home to deer, wolves, panthers, bobcats, turkeys, quail, and pheasant. Cranberries, grapes, and nuts grew wild, and the waters of the bay abounded in seafood and waterfowl. In addition to those bounties of nature, the Indians introduced the new settlers to a variety of foods that didn't exist in Europe—over forty in all—including pumpkins, kidney and lima beans, corn, tomatoes, potatoes, and squash. The Indians along the shores of Barnegat Bay were not only hunters and gatherers, but were also agrarian and skilled at rotating and fertilizing their crops. Every fall they held a festival of thanks to their god Manitou for their bounty of food, and the European settlers soon adopted this Thanksgiving celebration.

Waterborne commerce along the east coast of the United States in those early days was a natural result of its topography. The east coast is replete with inlets, estuaries, rivers, bays, and sounds, which makes it convenient for commerce by water. But large, commercial, square-rigged, ocean-going ships were unable to negotiate these narrow, shallow waterways and couldn't successfully beat to windward up the rivers and bays. It was then that the coastal schooner came into its own. The windward ability of the schooner's fore-and-aft rig and their shoal-draft enabled them to carry commerce far inland where square-riggers were unable to go. By the late eighteenth century, the schooner had become the national sailboat of the United States and replaced the square-rigger as the ship of choice for our coastal commerce.

The American coastal schooners were not deliberately designed to look beautiful; they were designed as vehicles of commerce, with good carrying capacity, able to haul passengers, fish, lumber, coal, ice, stone, bricks, fertilizer, and the like, in all possible weather and at good speed. Thus, a perfection of sail-plan and hull were developed, resulting in the rarity of something that was completely functional as well as aesthetically beautiful. They were as vital to U.S. commerce as are the highways, railroads, and airlines of today.

In those early days, before the railroads, when overland routes were not much more than muddy paths in the warm months and snow-covered ruts during the winter, schooners moved people and supplies along the coast when traveling or carrying freight by land was all but impossible. Access to these coastal schooners was vital to commerce and, as a result, all the major cities grew up along navigable waters.

By today's standards, travel in those days was primitive. A trip from the New Jersey shore to Philadelphia, which now takes less than two hours by car, would take two days by coastal schooner if the wind was right; or could take two weeks under adverse conditions—and there was always the possibility of never arriving at all if a nor'easter loomed up offshore.

As steam power advanced, railroads slowly began to replace the coastal schooners and travel by land became more practical. When those railroads reached the shore areas, the mainland towns were bypassed and the main attraction for travelers became the sun and surf on the barrier islands. As early as 1801, one of the first boarding houses on Absecon Island advertised rooms, "for entertaining company who use sea bathing."

For mariners, access between the ocean and Barnegat Bay has always been fraught with uncertainty due to the narrow, shallow inlets and breaking seas—and these inlets have always been in a constant state of change. In the 1750s, at the south end of Long Beach Island there was a single inlet, but within fifty years there were two: Old Inlet was still there, but Tuckers Island had formed, and just south of the new island was New Inlet. By 1890 Old Inlet had disappeared as Tuckers Island became part of the southern tip of Long Beach Island, and only one inlet, Little Egg Inlet, existed. But by 1920, Tuckers Island again became a true island with Beach Haven Inlet to its north and Little Egg Inlet on its south. By 1960, again Tuckers Island no longer existed and the "twin inlets" were side-by-side. Now Beach Haven Inlet is shoaling in and becoming part of Long Beach Island and only Little Egg Inlet remains as a usable inlet.

During the early 1900s, access to the New Jersey shore by land from the metropolitan areas of New York and Philadelphia was by train or by car. Those car trips could be daunting on weekends, however, since the narrow roads had a single lane in each direction. Things changed dramatically when the Garden State Parkway was proposed and came into fruition. Parkway construction started at the north and continued reaching farther south until, in 1954, it was completed all the way to Cape May. By the early 1950s the Parkway was completed to Ocean County, in which Barnegat Bay is located, and those living in congested northern New Jersey were finally able to travel to the Barnegat Bay area easily on weekends. During that decade, Ocean County's population increased by over 70 percent, and the last U.S. Census recorded a staggering 1,126,217 people now living in Monmouth and Ocean Counties—an increase of nearly 140,000 in the 1990s alone.

Obviously, as the population density increases, water quality becomes more threatened. Public awareness of the potential problems has led to the growth of environmental protection advocacy groups who serve as watchdogs for these waters. In the Barnegat Bay area alone there are: the Alliance for a Living Ocean (ALO), the Barnegat Bay Estuary Program, the Barnegat Bay Watershed Association, Clean Ocean Action, Rutgers University Extension Service, Save Barnegat Bay, the Trust for Public Land, among others. The dedicated professionals in all of these environmental groups, along with citizen-volunteers, have made noticeable strides forward in preserving Barnegat Bay, its surrounding wetlands, and the streams of its watershed.

In the spring of 1992, in an effort to develop and to monitor standards for the waters of Barnegat Bay, the New Jersey Sea Grant Advisory Service initiated the Barnegat Bay Watch Monitoring Program. This program, which is now under the auspices of the ALO, oversees ecological conditions in the bay. Its trained citizen-volunteers use their own boats to monitor water quality at specific locations throughout the bay, twice monthly, April through November. Equipment, supplied from grants, enables these volunteers to record pH levels, dissolved oxygen content, water clarity, water temperature, salinity, nitrates, and precipitation. Other information collected at each station includes water depth, bottom vegetation, weather conditions, tidal stage, surface conditions, water color and odor, and wildlife observations in and on the water. The information collected by the volunteers provides a database that aids in detecting episodic events and identifying trends or changes in water quality and habitats in the bay area.

Barnegat Bay is probably cleaner now than when I had my first sail in these waters in the 1930s; and perhaps through the efforts of these environmental organizations—and with the help of all of us—the waters of the bay can be saved for future generations, so our grandchildren and great-grandchildren will still find the New Jersey shore enticing.

South of Point Pleasant there are two different New Jersey shores: the narrow barrier islands that separate the ocean from the inland tidewaters; and the wetland shore of the mainland, to the west of the Intracoastal Waterway that snakes its way through the bays and sedges.

The main attractions for the majority of tourists visiting the New Jersey shore are the sandy beaches, the recreational activities, and the carnival atmosphere, all located on the barrier islands. While traveling to these meccas, tourists pass through the mainland shore communities with hardly a glance. However, it was the other New Jersey shore—the mainland—that attracted the first settlers to the area.

Years before the Europeans came to this land, the seasonal character of New Jersey's shore was understood by the Lenape Indians, who made a yearly migration to the shore from their encampments on the bluffs of the upper Delaware River. They hiked single-file down the narrow trails that led to the coastal waters. They were the first vacationers to come to the mainland shore of Barnegat Bay, where they caught crabs, fish, clams, and oysters.

For the first European settlers, the mainland side of Barnegat Bay was the most important, and few people went to the barrier islands except for hunting, whaling, or to graze their cattle. During the Revolutionary War, Barnegat's sailors set out from the rivers and streams that snaked up into the desolate pinelands off the bay to attack the British ships along the coast, returning easily through the familiar inlet shoals and bars of their home waters in their shallow-draft boats. No British captain of a square-rigger would have dared follow them. The British called the area "a nest of pirates."

For the cruising sailor of today, Barnegat's shores offer many facilities for transients. There are abundant marinas, restaurants at water's edge that can be visited by boat, and stores and transportation within walking or biking distance. If a relaxed time at anchor is part of your plan, many coves and rivers provide protected anchorages.

Nearly one-third of all of New Jersey's commercial docks, boatyards, marinas, yacht clubs, and public docks are located on the eastern and western shores of the Barnegat Bay region. In addition, hundreds of artificially constructed lagoons and private docks provide space for recreational craft. The estimate is that more than 50,000 boats have immediate access to these waters. On weekends and holidays water traffic can become intimidating. Paradoxically, during summer weekdays the bay is nearly empty.

As we travel south from Toms River into the 75 square miles of Barnegat Bay proper, we can see the Ferris wheel, roller coaster, and water slide at Sea-

Seaside Heights, as seen from the Intracoastal Waterway

side Heights to the east. There are several marinas at Seaside, and a few slips for transients are available for the small- to medium-sized craft.

The mile-long boardwalk at Seaside Heights and the wide beaches make it a natural for kids. There are rides, pinball and video games, fast-food stands, and arcades of all kinds.

The bay near Seaside is where I had my first sail. I was eight years old, and the year was 1934. My father, who had always had the romantic notion of skippering his own sailboat, had obtained a "how-to-sail" book from the library. Armed with his new-found knowledge, he took me and my brother and headed to Barnegat Bay, where he rented a catboat at Seaside Park. In the middle of the bay, book learning gave way to reality and we turned over, losing most of our clothes, all of our picnic gear, and our image of my father as a sailboat skipper. A power boat offered to pull us to shore, tied on to our bow cleat, and opened the throttle—we didn't move an inch. This was my first introduction to the amazing holding power of a properly set anchor; ours had fallen out of the cockpit when we overturned.

It was a bedraggled group of would-be sailors that arrived home that night. When my father saw my mother in the kitchen, he said, "If we sneak in the front door, we can get upstairs before your mother sees us." It didn't work. But I had had my first sail, and I was a goner. This was for me.

When I was eleven years old I built my first boat, all by myself. It was my own design and had all the nautical lines of a coffin. It didn't last long enough to get me in trouble, though, since the indoor plywood from which it was constructed delaminated the first season.

The second boat I built was made from a kit, a gift from my parents. I think they took pity on me. It was a wooden kayak, but I turned it into a sailboat, with a whittled-down two-by-four as a mast. My top-heavy boat could hold two very stable positions: one with the boat on its starboard side and the mast in the water, the other on its port side with the mast in the water. My boat was a good teacher, though, and after developing rapid reflexes, and while performing nimble feats of acrobatics, I could actually sail my boat for short periods of time between capsizes.

A quarter of a century later, I was the father, taking my son and daughter sailing on the bay. Now, seventy years after my first sail, our grandchildren are sailing with us on these same waters.

Just south of Seaside, in Berkeley Township, development on the barrier island stops. This is the north end of the 9-mile-long Island Beach State Park, where rolling scrub-covered dunes, more reminiscent of Cape Cod than the New Jersey shore, extend down to Barnegat Inlet.

Before this undeveloped beach became a state park, it played an important role during World War II. This strip of land was the site of a top-secret military project code-named Operation Bumblebee. An abandoned Coast Guard station was the base of operations for the project which, in 1945, produced the world's first successful flight of a supersonic guided missile, destined to change the face of military strategy.

After the war, when private home construction resumed, this barrier island was narrowly rescued from the decimation of bulldozers. Steel magnate Henry J. Phipps, owned Island Beach and dreamed of turning it into another Coral Gables, Florida, but in 1953, the land was purchased from his estate by the state of New Jersey and turned into a state park. An official shore-side residence for the Governor is near the north end of the park.

Island Beach State Park is one of many state parks in the Garden State. Although New Jersey is small, it has the third largest state park system in the United States.

Just south of the mouth of Toms River is Good Luck Point. The large brick building, surrounded by acres of masts that support transmitter antennas, was AT&T's Morse code ship-to-shore installation. Its receiving installation is a similar forest of masts farther down the bay, at Manahawkin.

On the southern tip of Good Luck Point, in the town of Bayville, just a few hundred yards off the Intracoastal Waterway at Mile 16, is The Water's Edge

Restaurant, which offers dining both inside and out. Thirteen slips are available for boaters, and reservations are recommended for dining but are not taken for the slips. Overnight use of the slips is not allowed. Since the restaurant's docks are adjacent to the ICW, wakes can cause problems for boats in the exposed slips.

A few miles farther south along the shore, also in Bayville, at ICW Mile 19, is Windows on the Bay, another restaurant that can be reached by boat. It offers a variety of excellent dishes and a splendid view of the bay. The small cove where the restaurant is located has deep water, but it becomes shallow as you approach the restaurant's dock. At dockside the water is about two and a half feet deep at normal low tide. The dock is suitable for small- to medium-sized craft, but deep-draft boats can anchor a hundred yards out and take the dinghy into the dock. Restaurant reservations are a good idea on weekends or holidays.

As we continue south, Island Beach State Park encloses the bay on the east. The park is one of the last unspoiled areas along our northern Atlantic coastline. Amidst the rolling dunes are holly, bayberry, pine, cedars, beach plum, and shore grasses. Walking through the dunes on other than the fenced-in paths is prohibited.

Tices Shoal, by Island Beach State Park

There's a designated anchorage on the bay side of Island Beach State Park called Tices Shoal, east of ICW Mile 23. It is easily identified during the summer months by the boats anchored close to shore. Here, boats with a draft of less than 5 feet can anchor in a bottom that has good holding, and the crew can swim, wade, or take a dinghy to shore and traverse the boardwalk across the island (about a quarter-mile) to an undeveloped ocean beach, while their boat remains safe in protected inland waters.

Some of our most cherished moments on the water have taken place when we've returned to our boat at Tices Shoal after spending a day on the beach. Supper eaten, we sit in the cockpit and watch the sun set behind the low mainland across the bay; the sky turns to shades of red and purple, and we listen to the ocean's boom and shear on the other side of the island.

As mentioned earlier, Barnegat Bay is a "No Discharge Zone." To aid boaters in emptying their holding tanks, there are pump-out boats on call to serve this purpose. One is frequently at Tices Shoal on weekends, but can also be summoned on your VHF radio from their base in Seaside.

Pelicans have recently migrated to this area during the summer months, and frequently, while anchored at Tices Shoal, we've seen a flock of brown pelicans flying north or south along Island Beach State Park. This is a strange sight at this latitude, as they're usually seen from North Carolina south.

The waters of Barnegat Bay are home to a large number of sailboats since, unlike the Chesapeake or Long Island Sound, it affords a good sea breeze during the summer months. The legendary Jersey mosquitoes, which were troublesome a few decades ago, are now largely controlled and will only be noticeable for about an hour at sunset. The same can't be said for the aggressive greenhead fly, the bane of boaters all along the east coast. From the middle of June until early September they can be a nuisance during daylight hours, mostly from Waretown south, and generally when the wind is blowing from the west. Repellents don't work well on these little monsters, and they don't mind going through heavy clothing to get their meal.

Precipitation and wind speeds on Barnegat Bay are at their lowest in July, with prevailing winds from the southwest from April through August and northeast winds during September and October. Wind directions and speed are modified by the daily sea breeze that starts in the late morning. It blows in off the ocean, created by the updraft from the warming of the mainland.

Tides on these inland waters (except when close to the inlets) run a foot or less. Of greater influence than the celestial tides is the wind. Strong, prolonged west winds cause very low *blow-out tides,* while onshore winds produce *blow-in tides.* This should be taken into account by skippers of deep-draft craft when they're planning an ICW cruise. During the prolonged

Aerial view of Barnegat Bay; the barrier island of Island Beach State Park is in the foreground and Forked River and Waretown are across the bay on the mainland shore (photo courtesy of Keith Hamilton, Studio-9, Waretown)

northeast winds of the December 1992 nor'easter, blow-in tides caused the bay waters to rise higher than they have at any time in nearly fifty years, flooding many homes and businesses.

The greater Barnegat Bay area, encompassing 47,615 acres, reaches from Toms River to the mainland town of Barnegat. It is the broadest and deepest part of New Jersey's inland tidewaters (chart 4.2). Despite its location, less than 100 miles from both New York and Philadelphia, Barnegat retains great charm. Each year ecological organizations are increasing the areas of undeveloped wetlands that border the bay through land purchases made by the National Wildlife Preserve. Small streams extend west into the Pine Barrens, and the bay waters teem with crabs, clams, and fish, making it an attractive spot for the recreational boater. Ocean beaches are a short walk across the barrier island, and yacht clubs, marinas, and restaurants are just a few minutes off the ICW.

There are many rivers, creeks, and streams that enter Barnegat Bay from the west. One of these streams, Forked River (pronounced For-ked), attracted

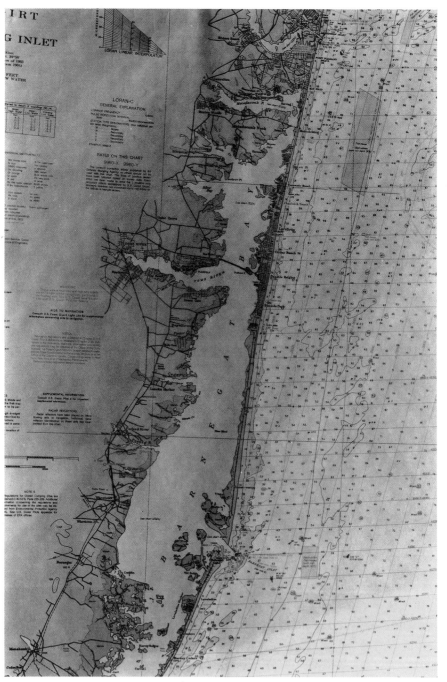

Chart 4.2 Barnegat Bay (reproduced from NOAA's Chart #12323)

Barnegat Bay Watch volunteers

the early settlers. After the Revolutionary War, Forked River's deep waters, its "hurricane-hole" qualities, and the fact that Barnegat Inlet was across the bay, made it a natural location for coastal trading schooners and fishermen, as well as for trips offshore to hunt whales. The town had food and lodging for the stage coach travelers along the sandy path that is now Route 9, and was a port of call for the coastal schooner trade. The calm bay waters, abundant with fish, crabs, and bivalves, eased the hard existence of the early settlers.

The town of Forked River has remained a flourishing fishing community, serving both recreational and commercial boaters. Its many large marinas provide access to wreck and artificial reef fishing offshore as well as to the bounties of the bay.

The river of Forked River is entered from Barnegat Bay at ICW mile 24. At center-channel tripod-shaped marker BB (which has octagonal panels of vertical red and white stripes and a white light flashing Morse letter *A* [dot-dash]),

The author's dock, next to his home on a man-made lagoon in Forked River

head west toward shore. Nearby you'll see flashing red New Jersey nun buoy number 2 that marks the entrance to the channel that leads into the river.

At the mouth of the river, to the north, is a large expanse of wetlands, and to the south, riverside homes crowd the banks. About a mile up from the entrance and halfway up to the head of navigation, the river separates into a south branch. Private homes are located a short way up the south branch, while farther up river it becomes the intake cooling water for the Oyster Creek Nuclear Power Plant. The warmed outlet water from the plant flows into Oyster Creek about a mile south along the bay. The 391-foot chimney of the plant is a landmark that can be seen far up and down the ICW. Residents of the area seem to coexist comfortably with the nuclear plant, which pays a large portion of the local taxes.

As we travel a little further up the north fork, the middle fork branches off to the south and is flanked by private homes and docks. The north fork provides all of the facilities of interest to transients: ten marinas with gas and diesel, repair services, haul-out facilities, pump-out stations, private and public launching ramps, and slips for transients.

A restaurant popular with both local boaters and transients, The Captain's Inn, is located on this north fork. The inn has many guest slips that are seldom filled, even on weekends or holidays. Showers are available, and transients can remain in a guest slip overnight for a fee.

Forked River

The Oyster Creek Nuclear Power Plant

At the head of navigation (about 2 miles from the bay), is the Forked River State Marina. It was built as a WPA project in the 1930s. In the new marina building there are showers and laundry facilities.

The marinas along Forked River's north fork are located on or near the major north-south artery of Route 9, providing access to buses that head south to Atlantic City and Cape May or north to northern New Jersey and New York City. This makes it a convenient spot for picking up or discharging passengers. From these marinas it is a short walk or bike ride to a boat-supply store, restaurants, a Laundromat, drug stores, food stores, the library, a motel, banks with ATMs, bait and fishing suppliers, ice machines, churches, and a variety of other stores and services located along Route 9.

For most of this century the area west of Barnegat Bay remained rural and the natives were called *pineys,* a term that is considered a badge of honor by the old-time residents. Recently, many new expensive homes have been built on the local waterways, slowly changing the character of the area. Almost gone are the days of the commercial fisherman, which are giving way to the recreational boater.

Sometimes the old-timers view the recent changes ruefully. Several years ago I was sitting in the old garvey of a weather-beaten and bearded piney clam-

The Captain's Inn on Forked River

mer. The paint on the hull of the boat was peeling, and the hardware was weeping rust. The grooves in the rails attested to many years of wear from a clam rake. We watched as the commissioning ceremonies of a newly-built yacht club got under way. "Them fellows gets all dressed up in them white uniforms," the clammer muttered, "but they don't know nothin' 'bout the water."

Each year, it seems, there are fewer of the honest old wooden work boats that, for centuries, have wrestled a livelihood from the bay and the sea.

At the mouth of Forked River, the ICW is just outside the entrance buoys, but if we're just interested in a peaceful lunch break or supper on board, we go along the undeveloped wetland shores just north of the river and drop the hook. Near the wetlands the water runs 5 to 6 feet deep, almost to shore, and we are protected from west winds. Be cautious of the water just to the south of the mouth of Forked River, which is very shallow.

If we're inclined, we might want to try fishing or crabbing. Harvesting clams or other mollusks from New Jersey's waters requires a license, and shellfish cannot be taken in condemned waters, from leased grounds, or on Sunday.

In the bays all along New Jersey's coastline the blue-claw crab is pursued by both commercial and recreational crabbers, and small wonder since,

Aerial view of Forked River looking down the river from the head of navigation (photo courtesy of Keith Hamilton, Studio-9, Waretown)

although this crab is always pugnacious, it is always delicious. All you need are some weighted handlines (with fish heads or chicken necks for bait), a net, and a basket, and you're ready for a fresh seafood treat. Don't fail to throw back crabs that are less that the legal width (four and a half inches point-to-point across the width of the shell for hard crabs) and females with eggs (visible as reddish roe clinging to the crab's underside).

A clammer at work on Barnegat Bay

In addition, there are, of course, seasonal, size, and number restrictions on several of the fish species in both the bay and the ocean. Contact the Marine Fisheries Administration or a bait store for more information.

Long before European settlers adopted Barnegat Bay's waters as their own, Native Americans used the bay as a nearly unlimited source of food.

In 1609, the Indians who camped along these shores had their first view of Europeans and their strange ships. In September of that year, Henry Hudson anchored his ship, *The Half Moon,* in the ocean just outside Barnegat inlet and sent a longboat through the inlet on an exploration mission into Barnegat Bay. On their return, the sailors reported seeing a sea monster in the bay. (It must have been a very shoal-draft sea monster.) The sea monster was described in the log of *The Half Moon,* where it was said to possess "three humps and a snake's head," and was seen "moving at the speed of a small boat." The sea monster wasn't seen again until 1935, when two fishermen anchored in the bay near Forked River photographed it; there is some question as to the photo's authenticity.

I can nearly guarantee, based on years of experience, that boaters cruising the bay will not be molested by sea monsters.

The busy Oyster Creek Channel, opposite Waretown, joins the ICW in Barnegat Bay with Barnegat Inlet and the town of Barnegat Light, at the north end of Long Beach Island. The juncture of Oyster Creek Channel and the ICW on Barnegat Bay is marked by pole-marker "BI." This *safe water* marker is mounted on a *dolphin* (a cluster of pilings lashed together).

For the transient who is unfamiliar with Oyster Creek Channel, a brief description will be helpful. The channel heads east from the juncture marker BI, and although well marked, navigational aids are uncharted. There's no room for error here. The channel is narrow, with shoals on both sides. Dog-leg turns in the channel can be easily overlooked and, even when properly executed, they can bring the boat broadside to the tidal flow—so looking over one's shoulder to line up the course is the rule. Every day during the summer we see someone aground outside the channel, waiting for a change of tide. The aerial photo of Oyster Creek Channel should provide enough information to warrant caution. If the unexpected happens, and you run aground and are either unable to get off or sustain damage, a call to Sea-Tow on the VHF radio (Ch-16) will bring a quick response. The nearest Sea-Tow is located in Barnegat Light and, as with all towing services, their time, which is usually over $100/hour, is calculated from the time they leave their dock till the time they return, so waiting for the next high tide to float you off is a money-saving endeavor.

Well before arriving at Barnegat Light, the Oyster Creek channel passes close to the south of several large sedges, which have been the site of a hunting lodge since before 1900. The lodge's excellent duck hunting and companionship attracted many notables at the time, including John D. Rockefeller Jr. and his wife Abby, as well as Babe Ruth, who enjoyed making clam chowder for the crowd at the nightly poker game. The building can be easily seen from Oyster Creek Channel.

After the passage through the tortuous twists, turns, and shoals, we arrive next at Barnegat Lighthouse. Here the marked waterway to the south takes us to the docks at the town of Barnegat Light, where marinas and an anchorage are convenient to both Barnegat Inlet and an offshore passage.

The channel heading out of Barnegat Inlet, takes us past the lighthouse, which is no longer operational and only shows a token light. The lighthouse is open to visitors and is well worth the climb up its 217 steps. There's a 32-acre state park surrounding the lighthouse; it's open to the public and offers picnic facilities, bathrooms, fishing in the inlet, and the opportunity to climb the lighthouse. The wire screen around the open platform at the top of the lighthouse helps prevent accidents, but its primary function is to eliminate the costly glass replacement on the dome, as migrating ducks and geese frequently crash into the tower at night.

There are restaurants, stores, a post office, ATMs and antique shops, as well as the ocean beach, within walking distance of Barnegat Light's marinas.

Aerial view of Oyster Creek Channel, which joins Barnegat Inlet with Barnegat Bay and the Intracoastal Waterway (photo courtesy of Keith Hamilton, Studio-9, Waretown)

For those who would prefer to anchor out, or for transients who enter through Barnegat Inlet to layover for the night, there is an anchorage basin just to the southwest of the lighthouse, with adequate water for deep-draft craft. It is a protected anchorage in nearly all wind conditions, with moderate tidal flow, and is a convenient spot to spend the night in anticipation of an early morning departure. You'll usually see one or more boats anchored there.

The first Barnegat Lighthouse was built in the dunes far from the inlet in 1834 and was illuminated by oil. Since New Jersey inlets have a tendency to migrate south, the lighthouse soon stood at the edge of the inlet and finally collapsed into the water in 1856. Construction on a new lighthouse (the present one), was started in 1857 and was completed a year later. Its walls are 10 feet thick at the base and 18 inches thick at the top, and the windows along the spiral staircase face different points of the compass. The original lens, made in France, weighed 5 tons, yet it could be turned by the pressure of one finger. It was rotated by a 150 lb. weight on 65 feet of rope inside the newel column of the spiral staircase, and it had to be manually wound up to the top

Barnegat Lighthouse

every hour. When constructed, it was the second tallest lighthouse in the United States. (The tallest was located in Pensacola, Florida.)

On August 15, 1927, the lighthouse was decommissioned and replaced by a lightship anchored 8 miles offshore. The lightship, the LV-79, couldn't be seen from any further out to sea than the lighthouse, and it required a fourteen-man crew in comparison to the three men who had been assigned to the lighthouse—a major step forward in efficiency. In 1928 her oil lamps were replaced by electric lights and in 1930 she was equipped with a radio beacon and fog horn. After the 1941 attack on Pearl Harbor, German U-boats began prowling the New Jersey coast and the lightship and crew became too vulnerable, so in 1942 the lightship was withdrawn from its station until after the war, when it again returned. New navigational technology, however, was making all lightships obsolete, and in 1967 the Barnegat Lightship was decommissioned.

An unusual event took place in 1951 after a May storm, when the lightship presented the Coast Guard with an unsolved mystery. After a May nor'easter, it was discovered that the heavy anchor chain had tied itself into a perfect overhand knot halfway between the anchor and the lightship. There was never any explanation, even from the Coast Guard, which only went so far as to explain in its *Coast Guard Bulletin*: "The anchor at one end of the chain weighs a ton or more. The ship, of course, is attached to the other." The tender *Sassafras* was able to raise the anchor onto its deck and eventually work out the knot.

Lighthouses, lightships, and buoys have marked the entrance to Barnegat Inlet for over a century and a half, and the attempts to keep the inlet navigable have continued from then to the present time.

A three year, multimillion dollar reconstruction and realignment of the south jetty of Barnegat Inlet was completed in 1991. This was an attempt to deepen and stabilize the inlet, which has always been considered one of the most dangerous on the East Coast. The newly finished south jetty juts out nearly a half mile into the ocean and, unlike the old one, is parallel to the north jetty. The area between the old and new south jetties is now a huge sandy beach. The design anticipates that the new jetty will create a flushing action that will deepen and maintain the inlet, a spot that has been notorious for its shallow entrance and breaking seas.

The government has been fixing Barnegat inlet ever since I was a child, but the inlet's nature has always been unstable and perverse. When transiting Barnegat Inlet it is always wise to use caution and, especially for the newcomer, to only do so when conditions are ideal. It is always easier to exit through the inlet than it is to enter. Steep seas build up near the mouth and, at low tide, even on relatively calm days, breakers can be encountered.

Aerial view of Barnegat Inlet, Oyster Creek Channel, and Barnegat Bay. The Oyster Creek Nuclear Plant is on the mainland in the distance (photo courtesy of Keith Hamilton, Studio-9, Waretown)

Another channel that joins Barnegat Inlet to the bay is located at a point farther south on the ICW, at Mile 28. This is Double Creek Channel; its twists and turns are marked but not charted. There are several shoal areas in the channel near the inlet, and it shouldn't be used at low tide by any boat with a draft of more than 2.5 feet.

On the mainland shore, in Waretown, one will find a restaurant at the Cape Island Marina. To visit the restaurant, take the entrance channel to the south of the large marina/restaurant building at water's edge. Slips for the restaurant are located just beyond the fuel dock and also around the corner to the right.

Due south of ICW marker 42, next to the shore of Conklin Island, there is a good anchorage for a meal aboard, a swim off the boat, or a quiet overnight stay, where the waters are protected from the prevailing south and west winds, but not from winds issuing from the northern quadrant. There is good holding here in a muddy sand bottom.

Just to the west of this anchorage is the marked but uncharted channel that leads into the old, historic, mainland town of Barnegat. Several marinas providing a complete range of services are just off the channel beyond the town dock, which is identified by the two-story open gazebo. Beyond that, a forest of masts identifies the largest marina in Barnegat, Mariner's Marina, which nearly always has slips for transients. Mariner's Marina offers a ship's store, a travel-lift, and a full range of repair services for hull, rigging, and engines. Its staff are especially knowledgeable about sailboats. The center of the quaint old town of Barnegat, where there are antique shops, a post office, and a fabulous turn-of-the-century ice cream parlor, is a long walk, or a short bike ride away (about 1 mile). A supermarket is in the other direction on Bay Avenue, a 2-mile ride from the marinas. The marina office provides telephone numbers for Chinese food and for pizza that can be delivered right to the marina, as well as information about restaurants within walking distance.

Throughout all of New Jersey's tidal waters there are opportunities for the curious cruiser to find interesting and protected *gunkholes*. Those new to boating are probably unfamiliar with this word, and it is one they can't find in most dictionaries. It is common usage in the lexicon of the inveterate cruiser, however, and can be used as either a noun or a verb. Gunkholing is the exploration of shallow, nearly unnavigable, and unmarked waterways and coves in search of seclusion, adventure, or wildlife.

From the wide expanses of Barnegat Bay, we'll now head further south on the ICW, through the narrow, shallow, and twisting waterway that leads to Atlantic City.

hapter Five

The Intracoastal Waterway between Barnegat Bay and Atlantic City

*M*ost of New Jersey's coastal residents use the name Barnegat Bay as an all-inclusive name to denote the waters from Bay Head to Beach Haven. Actually Barnegat Bay, as charted, comes to an end south of the mainland town of Barnegat. The bay waters between this point and Beach Haven, at the southern end of Long Beach Island, have the separate names of Manahawkin Bay and Little Egg Harbor. Although the government terms the waters of Barnegat Bay, Manahawkin Bay, and Little Egg Harbor as the "Barnegat Bay Complex," most boaters just call them Barnegat Bay. As mentioned in the last chapter the Barnegat Bay Complex is now a No Discharge Zone.

South of Barnegat Inlet is the 18-mile-long Long Beach Island. It is a family-oriented resort—no high rises here. There are many yacht clubs and marinas off the ICW, all along the bay side of Long Beach Island. From these facilities, it is a short walk to stores, entertainment, restaurants, or to spend a day on the oceanfront. Here, as on most of New Jersey's barrier-island beaches, beach badges (for a fee) are required when the guards are on duty, from Memorial Day to Labor Day. The badges can usually be obtained at the local municipal building or from the badge patrol on the beach; they can be purchased for the season, the week, or the day (and are frequently free to senior citizens). Rules for each beach, specifying those activities that are prohibited, are generally posted on a sign at the entrance path to the beach.

Water sports of all kinds exist on both the bay side and the ocean side of the barrier islands and include swimming, jet skiing, sailing, wind surfing, snorkeling, surfing, scuba diving, water-skiing, fishing, clamming, and motorboating.

Most residents of southern New Jersey, from Long Beach Island south, are

The Atlantic Coast Championship for the snipe class at Surf City Yacht Club on Manahawkin Bay. The yacht clubs on Long Beach Island host regattas and championships for many classes of small sailboats, with participants from all over the United States and occasionally foreign countries.

fond of telling people that they live below the Mason-Dixon line. The east-west portion of that line was established at latitude 39°43.325', and if it had extended through New Jersey, it would have crossed long Beach Island just south of Loveladies. The southern part of New Jersey is south of that latitude, but the line itself, the boundary between Pennsylvania and Maryland (established by surveyors Charles Mason and Jeremiah Dixon), was never extended through the Garden State.

Although it is speculated that Sebastian Cabot, an English navigator, may have been the first European to see Long Beach Island, there is very little documentation of his voyage. It appears that he explored the coast of North America from the Delmarva Peninsula north in 1498, on a futile voyage to discover the northwest passage, and it's likely his explorations included the coast of New Jersey. (The Delmarva Peninsula is a contraction of the names of the three states that share it, Delaware, Maryland, and Virginia.)

Giovanni da Verrazano was more probably the first European to see New Jersey's barrier islands, when he was on his way north along the coast in 1524. These narrow strips of land are characteristic of much of the Atlantic seaboard and the Gulf coast from Manasquan, New Jersey to the Mexican border.

In 1617, three years before the *Mayflower* pilgrims landed on Plymouth Rock, the Dutch were establishing colonies in the Barnegat Bay area. Whaling along the shores of Long Beach Island began in the mid-1600s. To aid whalers, a crow's nest was erected on the beach and used as a lookout. When whales were spotted, ships left the bay for the chase via the inlets, or boats were launched through the surf after the prey. When surf-launched boats killed the whale, it was towed back to shore, cut up, and rendered on the beach.

Although Long Beach Island was used by hunters, fishermen, and whalers even before the arrival of the Europeans, until train service began, just over a century ago, it could only be reached by boat. The railroad arrived at Long Beach Island in 1886. The low trestle across the bay at Manahawkin was frequently covered by storm tides and, finally, in the storm of 1935, it was washed away and was never rebuilt. The first road to the island (also a low causeway just a few feet above the water running parallel to the railroad bridge) was built in 1914 and remained in service until it was replaced in 1959. Now, a high, arching fixed bridge, with a 60-foot clearance, links Ship Bottom on the island with Manahawkin on the mainland. Tens of thousands of vacationers pour over this bridge during the summer months to enjoy the island's relaxed atmosphere and clean beaches. It is the only land link to the island.

The ocean beach on Long Beach Island

Boats that cruise the waters inside the barrier islands are almost completely safe from the vagaries of weather—almost, but not quite. Fortunately, hurricane and tropical storm forecasts now alert us well in advance and allow those on the water plenty of time for preparation. Not so with summer thunderstorms, during which winds can sometimes reach hurricane velocity and occur with little advance warning.

We have been on board sailboats during hundreds of thunderstorms, mostly when cruising the Caribbean and the southeastern states, and we've even been on the water when as many as three waterspouts at a time were just a few miles away (while sailing on the ocean side of the Florida Keys). However, our most violent experience in a thunderstorm took place in those benign, protected waters of New Jersey's inland bays, in Little Egg Harbor, off Long Beach Island.

We had anchored in the bay for a rendezvous with our friend John Fider, who tied his Sunfish to our stern and joined us for lunch on board. Just as we were finishing lunch the sky became dark and the wind shifted 180 degrees, a bad sign. We could hear the rumble of thunder over the mainland, and as John checked the line on his Sunfish, we let out more scope on the anchor and closed the ports and hatches. Suddenly John extended his arm and in a near-whisper said, "Look at that!" Across the bay the water had turned into a white froth as the squall line raced toward us. We all retreated into the cabin except for John, who wanted to experience the adventure in the cockpit. Then it hit.

We heard a large snap, and the boat went over 90 degrees, the top of the mast hitting the water. A tiny exposed section of our roller-furling Genoa jib had been grabbed by the wind, the huge sail unrolling to its fullest, knocking the boat over on its beam's end. As our son Tom and I struggled out of the cabin, the boat righted itself to about 45 degrees. John was not in the cockpit.

The lightning and thunder were simultaneous and, as we searched for John, the lightning flashes all around us were like glowing trees in the sky. The mixture of rain and hail, driven by the hurricane force winds, felt painful, even through our clothes. Finally, we heard John calling from behind the boat. I dropped the sail in the water, while Tom helped John back on board.

John later told us that when the wind hit, his Sunfish became airborne at the end of its tether and spun around three times, with the mast slashing through the water on each revolution. When our boat turned over, John couldn't hold on and fell out of the cockpit, but he managed to grab on to his Sunfish.

We discovered later that the anemometer at the Brant Beach Yacht Club nearby registered 75 miles an hour—hurricane force winds. Boats were overturned and, on shore, shingles were ripped from roofs and doors were torn from their hinges.

When the squall passed we assessed our damage. Surprisingly, our boat was intact, with no damage and no water in the cabin. The Sunfish had lost its daggerboard and life jacket, and the mast, a heavy 3-inch aluminum extrusion, was bent. We counted our blessings.

In sixty years on the water I had never experienced such a thunderstorm and, hopefully, I never will again. That night John and I spliced the mainbrace—and you can imagine how well we spliced it. So, let this be a caveat for anyone who ventures out on the water: don't take the weather for granted, even on the so-called protected waters inside the barrier islands.

Changes over the centuries have gently touched these intracoastal waters. As we continue our cruise through Little Egg Harbor, we find that our modern charts differ little from the charts first drawn by the early settlers.

Now we are nearing the southern end of Long Beach Island and the town of Beach Haven. There are large marinas and yacht clubs just off the ICW, along the southern end of the island. Here, there is access to shopping, restaurants, amusements, and the ocean beach, a short walk away. Beach Haven is the busiest and most densely populated town on the island. During the summer there is a large generation-X population (adults in their thirties and forties), and in the evening the neighborhood bars are jumping. But, there are plenty of attractions for the kids too. Fantasy Island, on West 17th Street, is a huge amusement park that provides entertainment for children of all ages.

On the ICW at Beach Haven, at red, flashing marker LB, there is a channel that leads into the deepest part of Little Egg Harbor and connects the ICW with Tuckerton on the mainland. From Memorial Day to Labor Day the "Waste Watcher" pump-out boat provides a free holding-tank pump-out service in the Little Egg Harbor Bay area. The boat is usually in service from Friday until Monday, and can be reached on VHF Channel-9.

Old-time Morse code shipboard radio operators from the first half of the last century remember the high-seas transmitting and receiving station at Tuckerton to be one of their few reliable links to the mainland.

The tower that provided this service was constructed by a German radio company, which began building in 1912 on Hickory Island off Tuckerton. The site was chosen for its firm ground, its unimpeded transmission of radio waves out to the Atlantic and toward Europe, and its soil, which was saturated with salt water and acted as an ideal radio-frequency ground plane. When the 853-foot tower was completed in 1914 (just at the beginning of World War I), it was the second highest construction in the world, next to the Eiffel Tower. Its intended purpose was trans-Atlantic communications as well as ship-to-shore service, and it was taken out of German management when the United States entered World War I.

Tuckerton has a history going back three centuries that belies the size of this small rural town. Its easy access to the nearby inlets, its protected waterway, and its proximity to mainland transportation, thrust it into importance even before the birth of our country.

Tuckerton, originally called Quakertown, then Fishtown, and finally Clamtown, was renamed after the Revolution by Ebenezer Tucker. Tucker was a member of Congress, who used his political clout to establish Tuckerton as the third port of entry into the new nation in 1791, under a commission from George Washington.

Although no longer a port of entry, Tuckerton's proximity to the Intracoastal Waterway and to Little Egg Inlet makes it a convenient home port for recreational craft.

There are numerous facilities for shoal-draft boats in Tuckerton Creek. Tuckerton Creek has had various names. The American Indians called it Pohatcong, and in the early 1700s it was known as Andrews Mill Creek, then Shrouds Mill Creek, Mill Creek, and finally, Tuckerton Creek.

On Route 9, at the south side of town, and at the headwaters of the Tuckerton Creek, is the Tuckerton Seaport. The Tuckerton Seaport's mission is to preserve the rich maritime history of the New Jersey shore. The 40-acre working seaport has exhibits of baymen's boats, decoys, and tools in the Lighthouse Museum as well as in the other twelve buildings that are on the waterfront. One of these is Skeeter's Seafood Cafe, which is open for lunch and dinner.

The Tuckerton Seaport can be visited by car or boat. The seaport's docks are located at the very end of Tuckerton Creek. Contact the dockmaster before arrival on either VHF Channel-88A or by telephone, (609) 296-8868. Slips are available from 10 a.m. to 4 p.m. in one of the seaport's twenty-seven floating docks, with assistance from the dockmaster and dockhands. Space is assigned on a first-come-first-served basis, and no overnight docking is allowed. All persons on board the vessel are required to pay the admission fee to the seaport, which includes your slip.

Back on the Intracoastal Waterway, we head south past the southern tip of Long Beach Island, where the ICW passes inside of Little Egg Inlet (chart 5.1). Although this is the southern extremity of the No Discharge Zone, it's probable that this restricted zone will be extended further south sometime in the future.

At the south end of Long Beach Island are two inlets that are side-by-side, Beach Haven Inlet and Little Egg Harbor Inlet. Beach Haven inlet is shoaling in and on its way to becoming part of Long Beach Island, and Little Egg Inlet is the only viable one now.

Strong winds from the southeast can send high waves through the inlet and across the inland waterway, making the trip uncomfortable or even

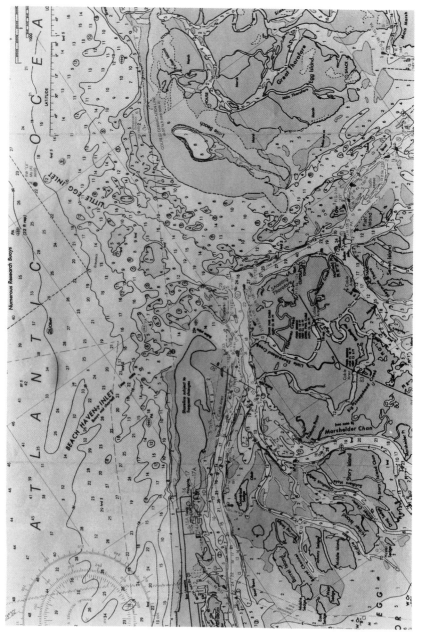

Chart 5.1 The twin inlets of Beach Haven and Little Egg (reproduced from NOAA's Chart #12316)

dangerous for small boats. For centuries the shoreline in this area has experienced drastic changes, and these changes continue. There are constantly shifting shoals within the inlets and along this exposed section of the ICW, especially after a storm. The ICW buoys in this area are frequently relocated and may not correspond to even the newest of charts.

When heading either north or south, don't confuse the buoys of Marshelder Channel, which leads toward Tuckerton, with those of the ICW. This can easily put you on a shoal, so newcomers should check the chart in this area carefully.

As the ICW makes a right turn to the west into Great Bay, the cupola on the chart at Shooting Thoroughfare indicates a building that was formerly a Coast Guard station and now houses the Center for Coastal Environmental Studies for the Marine Science Center of Rutgers University. The Building, which still retains the white siding and red roof of a Coast Guard station, is built on the low wetlands that, at high tide, frequently flood the land beneath the building and often make Great Bay Boulevard, which is the only access road, impassable. With funds from recent grants, improvements and expansion projects are under way at this facility that will provide high-tech ecosystem monitoring equipment, staffed by trained personnel.

The Marine Science Center of Rutgers University

Farther south, the ICW travels a small distance through the southeast corner of Great Bay. The channels here tend to shoal and change, and those in boats drawing over 4 feet should try to make the trip to Atlantic City on a rising tide. The waterway is especially narrow as it passes west of Tow Island, and staying in the center of the channel is a must, since there has been persistent shoaling there for years. Once, at this point, we met oncoming traffic in the narrow channel, and when cheating toward the edge of the waterway but while still inside of the markers, we ran aground—so take heed.

An interesting gunkhole can be found on a side trip up the Mullica River, whose entrance is in the northwest corner of Great Bay and is considered to be one of the least disturbed estuaries in the Boston to Washington, D.C., corridor.

Around the middle of the seventeenth century, Swedish immigrant Eric Mullica established a community along the Little Egg Harbor River and laid claim to a large parcel of land; but don't look for Little Egg Harbor River on the charts, it is now known as the Mullica River.

The Mullica River is rich in history. The iron bogs along its shores supplied Washington's army with cannon balls during the Revolution. This bog-iron ore, a hydrous peroxide of iron, was refined in huge charcoal kilns and was for years the chief industry in this part of southern New Jersey. Several miles up the Mullica River, the Bass River branches off to the north, where there are small craft facilities on both sides of the river in the small town of New Gretna (just before the bridge on Route 9 and the 20-foot fixed bridge on the Garden State Parkway).

One can gunkhole up the other tributaries of the Mullica: Nacote Creek, 4 miles from the Mullica's mouth, has 5 feet of water to the bascule bridge on Route 9, and then 3 feet to Port Republic; Wading River, 7.5 miles up the Mullica, has a water depth of about 4 feet to the bascule span at Route 542 (chart 5.2).

An interesting trip can be made up the Mullica to the head of navigation at Sweetwater. It is a trip that's popular with local boaters whose craft draw less than 3 feet and have mast heights that will clear the Garden State Parkway's 30-foot fixed bridge. This part of the Mullica is beyond the limits of the government chart #12316, but the channel is well marked by New Jersey buoys all the way to the headwaters. The charming inn, The Fork's, is appropriately located near a fork in the river, and about a half-mile before The Fork's one will find the Sweetwater Casino, another popular restaurant. Both eateries usually have dock space available, and fuel can be obtained at the Sweetwater Casino's fuel dock or at marinas further down the river.

This side excursion up the Mullica is representative; there are many

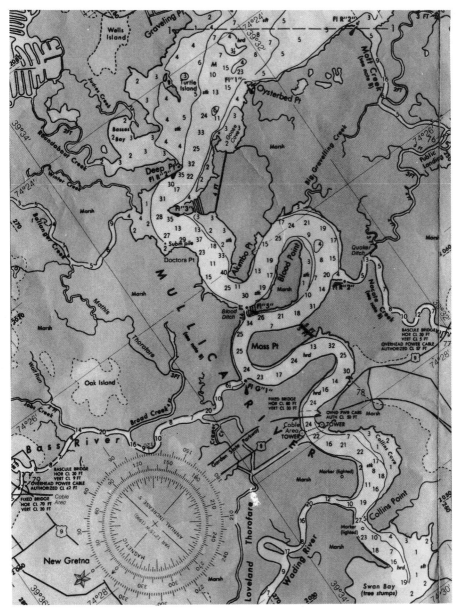

Chart 5.2 The Mullica, Bass, and Wading rivers (reproduced from NOAA's Chart #12316)

interesting possibilities for exploration that exist on the hundreds of rivers, creeks, and streams wending their way off the beaten track into the New Jersey wetlands and uplands. It would take a separate book to cover all these navigable waterways.

After this sojourn and back on the ICW, we will be able to see the tall buildings of Atlantic City across the wetlands of the Forsythe National Wildlife refuge at Brigantine (when the weather is clear). Refuge lands scattered along the shores of these waters comprise more than 30,000 acres of wetlands, making it the largest National Wildlife Refuge in the northeast region (thirteen states, from Canada to North Carolina), second only to the Great Dismal Swamp of Virginia and North Carolina. The Forsythe refuge is the home of a remarkable variety of shore birds and raptors, as well as the diverse waterfowl of the Atlantic flyway, wintering some 35 percent of the flyway's black duck population and nearly 70 percent of its Atlantic brants. The United Nations has listed the Forsythe habitat as one among only four sites in the U.S. originally included in its Wetlands of International Importance program.

Each year environmental organizations, in conjunction with the government, acquire new parcels of wetlands in an effort to preserve those last tracts of undeveloped shoreline. This effort is spearheaded by the Izaak Walton League, which relies on contributions and the Trust for Public Land for funding.

The TPL is a private, nonprofit conservation organization that works nationally to protect open space for people and wildlife. The TPL purchases endangered parcels and holds them temporarily until they can be resold to a government agency. This saves the government a tremendous amount of work and allows for effective use of the limited public money available. Once a refuge is established, the U.S. Fish and Wildlife Service (part of the Department of the Interior) is the governmental organization that oversees its operation.

Often on our cruises, we delve into our onboard library to read the history of the area we're passing through or to identify wildlife and waterfowl. From a lifetime cruising these waters, we are able to identify most of the species, but occasionally we're surprised by one that is unfamiliar.

On our southward path, the ICW cuts through the center of the Forsythe Refuge, a bird-watcher's delight. From the standpoint of bird-watching, early spring and fall are the best times for this trip, since the refuge is inhabited by huge numbers of migratory fowl. This is also the best time if one is concerned about creature comforts. During the summer months, in a slow boat and with the wind from the west, a trip through this area can be daunting. It is the policy of the refuge not to interfere with the procreation of any of the wildlife, including greenhead flies, and they can be a nuisance to summertime bird-watchers or to Atlantic City–bound gamblers. The only worse case of

The upper reaches of the Mullica River near Sweetwater

The Mullica River

The docks at the Forks Inn, near the head of navigation on the Mullica River

greenhead flies we've encountered plagued us when we were traveling the ICW through the Georgia savannas. My wife, Elsie, closed herself in the cabin while I did the swatting dance in the cockpit. I was itching to get away from there.

Nearly midway through the Forsythe refuge, a channel branches off the ICW to the east, which gives access to the shore town of Brigantine. Here, one will find a half-dozen small marinas with fuel and supplies. This channel is extremely narrow in spots—at times only 15 or 20 feet—and at the edge of the channel there is no water at all. If a visit by boat to Brigantine is on the schedule, it is best to use the channel further to the south; the entrance is just west of Atlantic City opposite buoy number 178.

In Atlantic City itself several marinas are available to the recreational transient in Clam Creek Basin, which is just off the south side of the inlet channel (chart 5.3). The largest of these is the Senator Frank S. Farley Marina, a public facility owned by the New Jersey Division of Parks and Forestry and managed by Trump's Castle Associates. Slips have shore power, water, telephone, and cable TV, and floating docks make getting on and off the boat much easier. Contact with the dock master is via Ch-65. The slips are easy to enter and have the advantage of not being affected by the tidal flow. Gas, diesel, and a pump-out station are available, along with a waste-oil disposal station, showers, laun-

The Forsythe Refuge, with Atlantic City in the distance

dry, a health club, twenty-four-hour security, as well as all the amenities one would find in a large yacht club. There is also a marina store that carries boating supplies, nautical clothing, and gifts. It also has a convenience-store section. The Harbor View Restaurant, a snack bar, and The Captain's Lounge are located in the marina building. Across the road is Trump's Castle (with casinos, restaurants, hotel accommodations, and shops). It is also accessible by a covered walkway. A jitney stop is located on the street between Trump's Castle and the marina building.

The jitney is Atlantic City's answer to San Francisco cable cars. Jitneys, at $1.50/trip, are available from the marinas to any of the casinos or a 2-mile ride to the boardwalk, eliminating the long walk through areas that some consider unsafe.

There are three smaller basins on the east side of Clam Creek Basin: Gardner Basin, Snug Harbor, and Delta Basin, where one will find several marine services. At the entrance to Clam Creek Basin, is Gardner Basin. In this area Atlantic City is creating a complex known as Historic Gardner's Basin, which includes a marina. The marina usually has a few transient slips available, with water and electricity, and the dock-master monitors Ch-9. Close to the marina are two restaurants: The Flying Cloud Restaurant and The Back-Bay Ale House. Also, don't miss the nearby Ocean Life Center, an aquarium and

The Sen. Frank S. Farley State Marina in Atlantic City (photo courtesy of Trump's Castle Associates)

A view of the Sen. Frank S. Farley Marina at night

marine-education center. Many summertime events are scheduled in this revitalized section of the city, and for the transient, the Jitney will take you to other parts of Atlantic City.

Kammerman's Atlantic City Marina is on the other side of Clam Creek Basin from the state marina. It offers slips for transients up to 75 feet, showers, a marine supply store, fuel, mechanics' services, and transportation to anywhere in Atlantic City. They monitor Ch-16. Since Atlantic City is a popular boating destination during the summer months, if a boat trip to Atlantic City is in your schedule, it's best to make an advanced reservation for a slip at the earliest possible date.

Atlantic City's boardwalk, the first in the world, was built in 1870 and now extends 4 miles along the ocean south of Atlantic City's inlet, Absecon Inlet. All along the boardwalk are small shops, amusements, food vendors and, of course, salt water taffy. There are several piers jutting out into the Atlantic along the city's oceanfront. The Steel Pier, in front of the Taj Mahal Casino, is an amusement pier, while Ocean One Pier, at the end of Arkansas Avenue and just north of the old Convention Center, is a mall, with stores, snack bars, and restaurants.

Casinos, both along the boardwalk and near the marinas, offer gambling, shops, and restaurants, along with big-name shows that rival those of Las Vegas.

Bathing attire on Atlantic City's beaches is a far cry from my first visit there in the early 1930s, when I was seven years old. Then, my brother and I were not allowed on the beach because our bathing suits didn't have tops.

In Atlantic City there are transportation connections by car, bus, rail (on Amtrak), or plane (to and from Atlantic City International Airport or Bader Field Airport, the municipal airport next to the ICW). By land it is about one hour to Philadelphia, two and a half hours to New York City and four hours to Washington, D.C. Although it is hard to conceive, nearly one-third of the population of the United States lives within 300 miles of Atlantic City.

The first Atlantic City entrepreneurs paid four cents an acre for the property where the city stands now. This was a bargain compared to the twenty-four cents an acre paid for property on the mainland. Now, that same twenty-four cents can't even buy one pull on the slot machine.

After the poorer and wiser crew has had their obligatory try at breaking the bank, we are ready to resume our cruise.

Heading south from Atlantic City, there are two options—or perhaps just one, depending on the boat. Boats with drafts of over 4 feet can expect to touch bottom more than once on the shallow ICW between Atlantic City and Cape May. With enough power they may be able to push themselves through the muddy

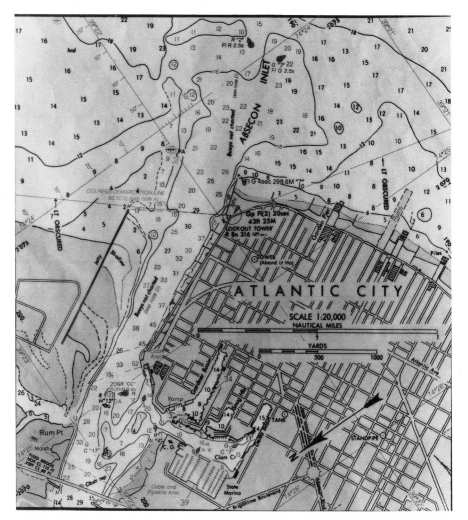

*C*hart 5.3 Atlantic City (reproduced from NOAA's Chart #12316)

bottom, however running aground or possibly causing damage to exposed propellers is always a possibility. Also, boats with masts of over 35 feet will be unable to make the inland trip at all, due to 35-foot fixed bridges across the Intracoastal Waterway. In boats restricted by draft or mast height, the trip south will have to be made in the ocean, by going out the Absecon Inlet and down the shore to the Cape May Inlet, formerly known as Cold Spring Harbor Inlet.

Atlantic City's inlet is wide, deep, and easy to use. The only warning here is to avoid the shoal area that extends well out into the ocean from the north jetty.

The Intracoastal Waterway route to Cape May is covered in the next chapter, and the offshore passage, the ocean trip to Cape May, is described in chapter 7.

Chapter Six

The Intracoastal Waterway from Atlantic City to Cape May and Cape May Ashore

*J*ust inside Atlantic City's Absecon Inlet, to the west of the highway bridge at ICW mile 65, the Intracoastal Waterway continues south past Atlantic City. As mentioned previously, the ICW between here and Cape May has limitations in mast-height and water depth. There are also numerous bascule bridges, both road and rail, with restricted opening times. It is no wonder that skippers of most medium-to large-size powerboats and skippers of nearly all sailboats do not consider this section of the Intracoastal Waterway as a viable route between Atlantic City and Cape May.

The ocean trip to Cape May from Atlantic City is 40 miles. Several of the inlets between Atlantic City and Cape May are marginal in good weather and shouldn't even be considered as a refuge during stormy conditions. When fog, high winds, or the threat of a storm is in the forecast and the safety of a trip down the coast is in doubt, the restrictions of the optional inside passage should be reconsidered. Boats with a draft of over 3 feet must remember that the nominal depths of the inside passage can be influenced considerably by blow-in or blow-out tides. After a prolonged west wind, the ICW will be shallower than normal, as much as a foot or more, as the inland water is blown out to sea; whereas, an east or northeast wind will provide a bonus in water depth but not in bridge clearance, as the ocean is pushed by the wind through the inlets into the intracoastal waters. If the weather is kicking up, the skippers of boats precluded from the inside passage by the ICW's limitations might well consider a day of boat-keeping, another try at the casinos, or a walk on the boardwalk. When planning any coastal or intracoastal cruise, it is wise to include a few buffer days for just such weather-related delays.

⚓ ⚓

There is no uniformity of opening hours for the bridges on the ICW between Atlantic City and Cape May—and this is by design. It was determined that this would allow ICW traffic to progress from one bridge to another with little delay if it traveled at a no-wake speed. Unfortunately, it seldom works this way.

As we head south past Absecon Island, on which Atlantic City is located, we pass Ventnor and then Margate, reaching the end of the Monopoly-board names. Ventnor and Margate have managed to remain relatively low-key in their principal function as suburbs of Atlantic City, and our trip along the waterway takes on a more residential flavor.

One of Margate's prime tourist attractions is Lucy the Elephant. This six story high wooden elephant, which overlooks the beach in this small residential community, was built in 1881 by land speculator James V. Lafferty. His hope was that the elephant would help lure real estate buyers to that area, which was then called South Atlantic City. In the early 1900s, the 90-ton structure became a private home, and later a rooming house, before it was finally converted into a tourist attraction.

As we leave Absecon Island behind, we come to Great Egg Inlet, which separates Absecon Island from the next barrier island where Ocean City is located. To the west of the inlet are the waters of Great Egg Harbor.

There are several marinas off the ICW at Ocean City, and they welcome transients. Typical of these is the huge Seaview Harbor Marina and Islander Restaurant, with slips for transients, fuel, pool, showers, car rental service, pump-out, and repair facilities. It is just to the north of the inlet, before the fixed bridge and monitors both Ch-10 and Ch-16. Other marinas are scattered along Ocean City's inland waterfront.

Ocean City caters to families, especially toddlers. The Wonderland Pier at 6th Street and Playland at 10th Street provide fun for kids and, of course, there is always Ocean City's clean beach. In the summertime Ocean City's population soars to more than 125,000. To get away from the crowds, try Corsons Inlet State Park at the tip of the island.

The Ocean City Coast Guard station cannot be seen from the ICW, except for its tall flagpole. The station itself is tucked into a sort of cul-de-sac off the main channel.

When listening to the weather channels on the VHF-FM Marine Band, one will frequently hear forecasts given for Ocean City. These forecasts often refer to the other Ocean City, Ocean City, Maryland, which is located on one of the barrier islands of the Delmarva coast, 42 miles south of Cape May. Since this part of Maryland is included in many of the local weather forecasts, don't be misled into thinking that the reference is to Ocean City, New Jersey. Unfortunately the weather service never seems to differentiate between the two Ocean Cities.

New Jersey's Ocean City was established as a dry town by the three Lake brothers, all Methodist ministers, who purchased the land in 1879, and some of their original restrictions on liquor sales are still written into the deeds today.

In present-day Ocean City, New Jersey, there are several residential marinas, that is, co-ops or condos with boat slips included. For several years now, marina owners have found it more profitable to close down their marina operations and to build complexes of this type; the trend is seen throughout the nation's waterways. Many times, when looking for a once-visited boatyard, we've discovered that it's been replaced by one of these non-public facilities.

Just south of Great Egg Harbor Inlet, at Ocean City, a marked waterway branches off the ICW heading west to Somers Point, less than 2 miles away, where there are small-craft facilities with fuel, marine repairs, haul-out, shops, and restaurants along the waterfront. At Somers Point, overlooking Great Egg Harbor, is a beautiful park and a well-maintained public launching ramp and parking area. Just beyond this park, at the west end of Great Egg Harbor, Tuckahoe River and Great Egg Harbor River provide interesting side trips. Both of these deep rivers wend their way through the wetlands into higher and more populated areas. The Great Egg Harbor River is navigable for 15 miles, to Mays Landing, and the Tuckahoe Rover for 7 miles to Tuckahoe. One can also explore Patcong Creek, Cedar Swamp Creek, Middle River, or Powell Creek, all on the western end of Great Egg Harbor.

A trip up the Great Egg Harbor River to the town of Mays Landing makes a wonderful day's outing. Although not charted, the waterway is well marked with buoys all the way to the harbor at Mays Landing. For the first few miles this tidal stream winds through wetlands that have not changed in hundreds of years. Here the river is wide and deep. Finally, as we approach Mays Landing, the banks become higher and more populated as the river narrows. In Mays Landing we find a cozy little harbor with marina facilities and public docks.

In 1740, Captain George May, an agent for the London Company, sailed up the Great Egg Harbor River and found a region rich in oak and pine—a perfect ship-building location. A few years later he bought property near Babcock Creek, which flows into the northwest end of the Mays Landing Harbor, and established a trading post and shipyard. By 1778 the area began being called Mays Landing.

In the late 1700s sugar, molasses, and rum were brought up the river and stored on a grassy knoll at Mays Landing, awaiting shipment by horse and cart to Philadelphia. The knoll became known as Sugar Hill. About 1846 William

Moore, a state senator, who managed a fleet of trading vessels, built a mansion on Sugar Hill. In 1986 the mansion was restored and became the Inn at Sugar Hill. The Inn has a dock at the foot of the rolling lawn that leads down from the mansion, where boaters can dock and savor their excellent cuisine. This alone makes the trip up the river worth while. From the public docks in the harbor, the dock at the Inn, or from the marina, it's a short walk into the town of Mays Landing.

As we return to the Intracoastal Waterway and resume our trip south I'm reminded of one of our first trips through these waters. Many years ago my wife, Elsie, and I, along with our son Tom, were bringing a small sailboat up from the Florida Keys to New Jersey. It was the spring of the year and the ocean was still acting temperamentally. At Cape May, the offshore trip looked marginal for the type of craft we were sailing. Our boat's mast was just over 37 feet, nevertheless we elected to try the inside passage through the three 35-foot fixed bridges.

As we approached the first fixed bridge, the clearance marker along the bridge abutment showed 35.5 feet; we needed to reduce our height by a foot and a half. Tom fastened himself to the end of the boom in a bosun's chair, and we swung him out over the water. Then, with both Elsie and I hanging over on the same side, we were able to heel the boat over just enough to make

Negotiating the fixed bridges, with Tom out on the end of the boom

it through. We performed the same maneuver at each of the 35-foot fixed bridges, until finally arriving at Atlantic City. I'm sure we presented an entertaining diversion for the people on shore.

As we continue south, the ICW now picks its way through sedges and marshlands to the west of Corson Inlet. At ICW pole number 328 a marked waterway heads off to the east. Following this side channel to Strathmere on the barrier island a mile and a half away, we find several marinas with fuel, marine supplies, and repair facilities.

Sea Isle City is on this same barrier island. A railroad line reached Sea Isle City in 1884, and the city burgeoned as a mecca for Philadelphia vacationers. At that time, the tracks were built through Sea Isle City to Townsends Inlet at the south of the island and, in 1889, two railroad draw-bridges were constructed across Townsends Inlet, leading to the city of Avalon, on the island to the south, Seven Mile Beach.

In the last few years Sea Isle City has become popular with the younger crowd, teenagers and adults between the ages of twenty and thirty. The area also boasts a large commercial fishing industry, which is reflected in the numerous seafood restaurants and fish markets on shore.

Just off the ICW, at Avalon, there are three channels that head east off the waterway: Cornell Harbor, Pennsylvania Harbor, and Princeton Harbor. Although the ends of these harbors are connected by water along Avalon's waterfront, they are crossed by fixed bridges with just a few feet of clearance, preventing their use by anything but very small boats. One of the several marinas at Avalon is the Commodore Bay Marina, just south of the Townsends Inlet bridge, at the end of Cornell Harbor. It monitors Ch-16 and welcomes transients. The Avalon Pointe Marina is located a little further south, on the west bank of the ICW. It offers a full line of services, welcomes transients, and also monitors Ch-16.

At this point, the ICW passes close to the town of Stone Harbor, where residential homes dominate the waterfront. On the northwest side of the bascule bridge at Stone Harbor one will find the Stone Harbor Marina.

About a half-mile down the road, to the west of the marina and the bascule bridge (and, appropriately, in the wetlands), travelers will discover the attractive cedar-shake building housing the Wetlands Institute. The institute offers educational programs and a coastal museum, with exhibits for young and old. It is a private, nonprofit organization supported by gifts and donations. Its calendar of both indoor and outdoor programs provides diversions and education for everyone, from the toddler to the serious adult environmentalist. The lobby of the institute offers a gift shop as well as a book store with a huge variety of books on wildlife and ecology.

The Wetlands Institute at Stone Harbor

The waterway now passes Wildwood and Wildwood Crest. Sunset Lake is a comparatively deep harbor next to Wildwood Crest, and either of the two charted entrances can be used.

Through the years, the character of the Wildwoods has changed markedly, from a wooded barrier island of little economic value to the bustling, popular oceanside resort of today. The land now called Wildwood and Wildwood Crest was sold by its owner, in 1700 or thereabouts, for nine pounds; he used the money to buy a calico dress for his wife.

Almost two centuries later, in 1890, Philip Baker, a state senator from Cumberland County, purchased 100 acres. At that time the property was a thick forest of oaks and cedars, with wild grapevines climbing to the treetops. Beneath the canopy, moss and wildflowers hung from the branches, and huge huckleberry bushes grew on the forest floor. It was truly a wild wood; Wildwood was an appropriate name. This didn't last long, however.

In 1912 an automobile bridge was built across the wetlands to Wildwood, and a boardwalk was constructed, making Wildwood an amusement center. Property was parceled off and Wildwood, along with the wild woods, had the dubitable distinction of being propelled into the twentieth century. Today, the boardwalk along Wildwood's wide beaches is an attraction for those seeking rides, fast food, T-shirt shops, and an amusement-park atmosphere.

The Hereford Inlet Lighthouse

In North Wildwood, close to Hereford Inlet, is the quaint Victorian-styled Hereford Inlet Lighthouse, which was built in 1874. The lighthouse, on a sand dune overlooking the inlet, is no longer operational. In 1982 it was restored and its original fourth order lens put on display. The lighthouse was turned over to the town of North Wildwood and now serves as a museum, maintained by the Hereford Inlet Lighthouse Commission and community volunteers.

At Wildwood Crest, just north of the Cape May Inlet and Cape May Harbor, one will find the Two Mile Landing Marina. It monitors Ch-16 and has slips for transient boats that are up to 100 feet long, with a good approach and dockside depth, along with two restaurants. Skippers of large powerboats, or of sailboats that are unable to use the ICW south of Atlantic City, can reach the marina by going a short way north from Cape May Harbor or Cape May Inlet. The marina can easily be seen off the ICW to the east after passing through the bascule bridge at the north end of Cape May Harbor. Whenever marinas in Cape May Harbor are booked solid, and hanging on the hook is not appealing, this marina, which is off the beaten track, is worth investigating. For those who would like to anchor out, the deep waterway between the ICW and the Two Mile Landing Marina is a quiet and protected location. From here it is not too far to take a dinghy with an outboard into Cape May for supplies.

A few miles farther south the waterway passes inside of the Cape May Inlet, entering Cape May Harbor and marking the southern end of the New Jersey Intracoastal Waterway (chart 6.1). The best is saved until last.

The harbor at Cape May is a cozy one, completely protected from storms. There are three narrow entrances to the harbor: the ICW to the north, the Cape May Inlet to the east (which is one of the best on the New Jersey coast), and the Cape May Canal leading to Delaware Bay on the west. The harbor is a popular layover spot for boats waiting out bad weather before heading in one of three directions: west across Delaware Bay, north up the Atlantic coast to Atlantic City or beyond, or south on the ocean side of the Delmarva, toward Chesapeake Bay. A layover here is a good excuse, if one is needed, to enjoy the pleasures of this southern tip of New Jersey, which few realize is south of Baltimore, Maryland.

If possible, it's a good idea to make reservations at one of the numerous marinas or yacht clubs here; when fishing tournaments are held offshore, slips for transients don't exist. It is possible, though, to anchor well off the channel in the harbor and take the dinghy in to shore, where most of the places of interest are within walking or biking distance. Due to its flat terrain, Cape May is an ideal walking or biking area, and if there are no bikes on board, they can be rented at some marinas and several other locations on shore.

The town of Cape May, with its Victorian architecture and meticulously

The Coast Guard station in Cape May Harbor

Cape May Harbor

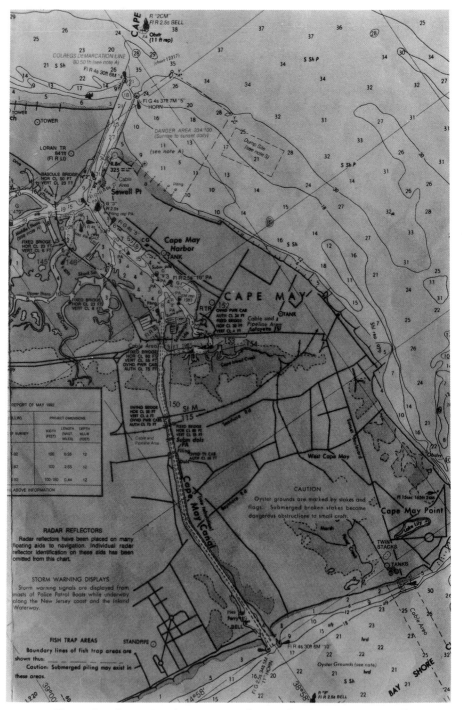

Chart 6.1 Cape May (reproduced from NOAA's Chart #12304)

kept homes, has been declared a national historic landmark. Much of the town has changed little since the end of the last century. It is hard not to fall in love with Cape May, and a tour makes a fascinating excursion. The oceanfront is two miles away from the harbor, and an outdoor pedestrian mall is somewhat closer. The immense sea wall along Cape May's waterfront was built after the devastating nor'easter in the spring of 1962, which wreaked havoc all along the New Jersey coast and flooded most of the city.

One will find that many of the old Victorian homes in town, especially those along the oceanfront, have been turned into bed-and-breakfasts, where reservations are necessary during the summer season.

Cape May is proud of its history, and the past still pleasantly flavors the town's ambiance. In a time when new, modern accommodations are venerated and the word old is usually meant as a condemnation, it is refreshing to visit Cape May.

Going back in time, the first permanent European settlers at the cape were New England whalers, who arrived in the mid-1600s. Travelers from Philadelphia were the first to use Cape May as a vacation resort, arriving by steamboat and sailing packet from the Delaware River and Delaware Bay in the early 1800s. Access to Cape May in those days was primarily by boat, since the roads

The Victorian homes of Cape May

to the cape remained wretched. A railroad finally terminated there in 1863, adding impetus to recreational development.

When the Garden State Parkway arrived in Cape May in 1954, it was feared the town would succumb to glitter and glitz, which usually results from easy access. Fortunately, it has remained essentially quaint, and the glitter and glitz seekers must find it elsewhere.

If the opportunity exists, we never miss the Cape May State Park, 4 miles from the harbor (taking Sunset Boulevard west, then Lighthouse Road off to the left). Cape May Point Park is one of the most popular bird-watching sites in North America. It is on the Atlantic flyway, the natural route of migrating birds that head north or south in the spring and fall, and it is also a wetland area that provides refuge to flocks awaiting good weather for the Delaware Bay crossing or for nesting or recuperation after the crossing. During the spring and autumn migrations more than 360 species have been counted, and it is common both at Cape May Point and in Cape May proper to see field glasses aplenty. Guided bird walks are given at the park; bird-watching platforms have been erected; and there is a nature museum close to the lighthouse. The park offers 3 miles of trails and boardwalks, and self-guided nature trail information is available at the park office. Surf fishing is permitted, and picnic sites with tables and grills are provided.

The World War II artillery bunker off Cape May Point

On the beach at the park, just beyond the breakers, one will find a World War II concrete artillery bunker that, when built in 1942, was located on a high sand dune 900 feet inland. The bunker's armament consisted of four 155 mm cost artillery guns and several 6-inch guns. Its walls and roof are made of 6-foot-thick reinforced concrete. A sister bunker, built to guard the cape at the southern entrance of Delaware Bay, stands firm at Cape Henlopen near Lewes, Delaware.

The old trolley tracks that went south from the town of Cape May to the town of Cape May Point, which were in use from 1892 to 1918, are now at the bottom of the ocean about a quarter-mile offshore. Both tracks and bunker provide a dramatic example of the changeable nature of the shoreline along this southern tip of New Jersey.

This rapidly changing shoreline has taken its toll on lighthouses at the cape. The first lighthouse was built in 1823, but soon the sea encroached on its base; it was undermined and collapsed. The second one, built in 1847 about 600 yards from the present lighthouse, suffered the same fate. The lighthouse that now stands at the park was erected in 1859. It is 170 feet high, with walls 8 feet thick at the base and, for the foreseeable future, it seems to be safe. The lighthouse is open to the public. It is a climb of 199 steps to the top, where a spectacular view of New Jersey's southern cape awaits. In 1933 the lighthouse became automated, and in 1940 its first-order Fresnel lens was removed and

Cape May Lighthouse

eventually put on display at the Cape May County Historical Museum. Today the light at the lighthouse has a reflector lens and uses a 1,000-watt electric bulb. The Cape May Lighthouse is only one of two along the New Jersey coastline that are still navigational, the other being the Sandy Hook Lighthouse.

At the end of Sunset Boulevard in Cape May Point is the Delaware Bay Beach called Sunset Beach. Near the beach are the remains of the freighter, *Atlantus,* which was built of concrete (due to the steel shortage during World War I) by the Liberty Shipbuilding Company in Wilmington, Delaware. From this bay beach one can see the major shipping on Delaware Bay's main channel and the ferries going back and forth between Cape May and Lewes (pronounced "Lewis"), Delaware. On a clear day, when standing on a sand dune, one can see the low coastline of Cape Henlopen, Delaware, 17 miles to the south. Since this beach is on the bay, waters are calmer and safer and can be enjoyed by small children.

Aerial view of Cape May Point. In the foreground are the town of Cape May Point and the Cape May lighthouse. Beyond that we see a Cape May–Lewes ferry that is entering the Cape May Canal, and far in the distance we can see the north shore of Delaware Bay (photo courtesy of Keith Hamilton, Studio-9, Waretown)

On all of Cape May's beaches one can have fun looking for the so-called Cape May diamonds. These small quartz, semiprecious stones come in all sizes, and many of Cape May's stores sell them polished and cut or mounted in jewelry. At Sunset Beach it won't take long to find one.

Some other points of interest near the town include the Coast Guard's basic-training center; the Cape May Historical Museum, at Cape May Courthouse on Route 9; and a 128-acre zoo at Cape May County Park, about ten miles north of town.

There are several restaurants close to the harbor and many more near the center of town, and there is a Wawa store just a short walk from the harbor. A supermarket is in town, a short bike ride or long walk away. A particular favorite of boaters is the Lobster House, located next to the commercial fishing docks at the southwest end of the harbor. It is a restaurant we always visit during one of our cruises. It has an outdoor raw-bar, a large inside dining room overlooking the water, a seafood store with an unbelievable selection, and a cocktail bar aboard the vintage Grand Banks schooner *American* (no relation to the schooner *America* of America's Cup fame), which is at dockside next to the restaurant. The restaurant's decor includes model ships, half-hulls, old photographs, and newspaper articles that recall the area's fishing heritage.

The property adjoining the Lobster House is occupied by Utsch's Marina, a family-owned-and-operated business. It has slips for transients, fuel, a large marine store, showers, a travel-lift, and it can handle hull and engine repairs. The marina entrance can be reached by turning 90 degrees at ICW flashing-red number 14, and then proceeding about 20 feet off the marina's bulkhead to the entrance. Alternately, it can be entered by heading south off the ICW toward the fishing docks at flashing-red number 10, passing between buoys numbered 1 and 2, and proceeding to the marina entrance. This latter approach should only be used by skippers of shoal-draft craft. Skippers of deep-draft boats should check with the marina for approach depths if there is any question. The marina monitors Ch-16. Utsch's Marina is representative of the several fine marinas in Cape May Harbor.

When it's finally time to say a reluctant farewell to Cape May Harbor and to continue on our cruise, several options present themselves. At the northeastern corner of Cape May Harbor, we can take the Intracoastal Waterway—the inland route we described earlier in this chapter. Also at the northeastern corner of the harbor is Cape May Inlet, which is our access to the ocean and an ocean trip north toward Atlantic City, Sandy Hook, and New York Harbor, or south to the entrance of Delaware Bay. The more venturesome can use the Cape May Inlet as a jumping-off point for an ocean trip outside the Delmarva

Utsch's Marina in Cape May Harbor

The Cape May Canal

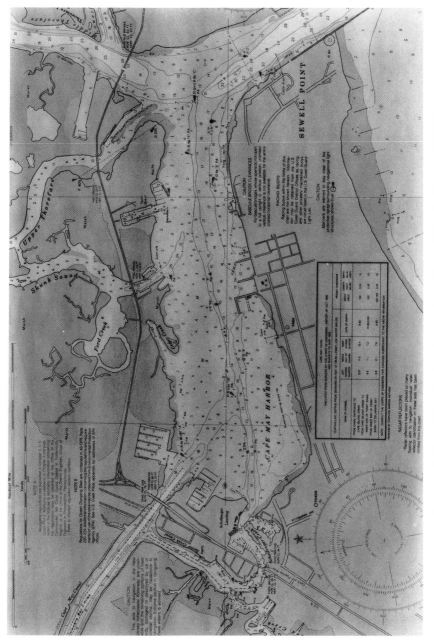

Chart 6.2 Cape May Harbor (reproduced from NOAA's Chart #12317)

Peninsula, to the Chesapeake and beyond, or even as a rumb-line to the eastern tip of Long Island and on to New England waters.

At the southwestern corner of Cape May Harbor is the entrance to the Cape May Canal, which joins Cape May Harbor with Delaware Bay—the bay being on the western shore of the Cape May peninsula (chart 6.2). There are several opportunities for gunkholing the small streams off Delaware Bay or one can travel to the Chesapeake and Delaware Canal, which leads to the north end of Chesapeake Bay. One can also go past the Chesapeake and Delaware Canal and follow the Delaware River up to its head of navigation at Trenton.

In the next chapter we will look at the alternate way of reaching Cape May, the offshore passage. Then in chapter 8, we'll explore Delaware Bay and its tributaries.

Chapter Seven

The Offshore Passage: Manasquan Inlet to Cape May

*T*he previous chapters have dealt with the inside passage, New Jersey's Intracoastal Waterway from Manasquan Inlet to Cape May. Some boat owners, under the constraints of high masts, deep keels, or time, will be unable or unwilling to take this leisurely shoal-draft route south. For them, the offshore route along the New Jersey coast is the alternative.

In chapter 3, I discussed the offshore trip from Sandy Hook down the coast to Manasquan Inlet and through the inlet into the Intracoastal Waterway. Now, let's take a look at the ocean trip from Manasquan Inlet south to Cape May.

The distance by ocean from Manasquan Inlet to the Cape May Inlet is 85 nautical miles (98 statute miles). For a boat leaving from Sandy Hook and taking the ocean route to Cape May, the total distance is 127 statute miles. It is obvious that displacement hulls, such as most sailboats and trawler-type powerboats, will be unable to complete this trip down the coast of New Jersey during daylight hours, even under ideal conditions. If a nighttime stopover on inland waters, using one of the inlets, is not planned, a crew competent in night passages and able to stand watches will be necessary.

It should be remembered that electing to take the ocean route doesn't limit one's options; a combination of offshore and inland passages can be taken, depending on weather and personal interests.

Those traveling in high-speed powerboats will have to calculate the time it will take for the offshore trip according to the expected boat speed; but remember that this boat speed could be severely compromised by wave conditions. One advantage of traveling in a high-speed powerboat and using the ocean route is that speed is not restricted by the numerous no-wake zones that exist on the ICW. For the sailor, there is a greater opportunity to hoist sail on the offshore passage, and the constant sail trim and the delays for bridges that one encounters on the ICW is eliminated. Another advantage to the offshore route is that the nearly straight-line passage is about 15 miles shorter than the passage along the ICW route between Manasquan and Cape May. In a displacement-hull craft this can easily save travelers two hours or more.

A disadvantage to this offshore route is that one must factor into the equation the possibility of changing weather conditions. If the weather starts kicking up, is the boat seaworthy enough to continue the passage safely? Will its draft restrictions make it unable to enter one of the inlets? Will there be a safe inlet nearby if weather conditions deteriorate? These are important considerations since, when the weather gets rough, many of New Jersey's inlets become dangerous and cannot be used. Are we familiar enough with the boat to know how it will handle in rough seas? Is the engine in good shape, and is there enough fuel for the planned passage? We must always keep in mind that the ocean, like a mischievous child, doesn't like to obey the rules and frequently does the unexpected. It doesn't hurt to look at weather forecasts with a jaundiced eye.

Storms and shipwrecks along the New Jersey coast have been a fact of life since the days of Henry Hudson's explorations. No one knows how many ships have been violently delivered onto the beaches of New Jersey, but the estimates are several thousand, probably one for every few hundred yards along our shoreline. In one stormy month, during the winter of 1826–27, more than two hundred ships were wrecked on these shores. These wrecks provided unexpected bounty for the poor fishing families that lived along the coast, and there is even some evidence that ships were enticed ashore with false signals sent by the so-called wreckers or mooncussers on land.

From the standpoint of the onshore salvager, one of the more memorable shipwrecks occurred in the spring of 1897. The two-masted sailing ship *Francis,* having sailed out of California with a full cargo, was being driven ashore on Long Beach Island. Seeing that the ship's destruction was near, the island residents launched their surf boats and rescued all twenty-five persons on board just before the *Francis* was grounded in the surf line and began breaking up. When the cargo started drifting to shore, word spread throughout the island and every resident headed for the beach. Some crates that drifted ashore contained food, but the major part of the cargo consisted of barrels of California wine, port, sherry, Madeira, brandy, and crates of bottled champagne. A beach party ensued that lasted two days—it was truly a tight little island. By the morning of the third day an island-wide hangover epidemic ensued, and things quieted down considerably. The cargo was listed as lost at sea.

During both world wars, it wasn't only the weather but German U-boats that sent ships to the bottom along our coast. Older shore residents remember the many nights that tankers and freighters could be seen burning offshore. For years, the high water mark on New Jersey beaches was edged with black oil.

Three of the worst storms to visit the New Jersey coast in this century were the 1944 hurricane, the 1962 spring nor'easter, and the nor'easter of December 1992. In each of these storms wind-blown waves washed across the barrier islands, and the inland bays rose to unprecedented heights. Although hurricanes are what everyone dreads, it is frequently the prolonged nor'easters that do the most damage along this coastline.

Now, let's leave the talk of storms and shipwrecks and take a calmer look at the offshore trip from Manasquan south to Cape May.

The principle improved inlets along the New Jersey coast, that is, those with breakwaters and dredging programs are: Shark River, Manasquan, Barnegat, Absecon (Atlantic City), and Cape May (formerly Cold Spring Harbor Inlet). The other, unimproved inlets are best used while employing local knowledge and extreme caution, or not at all. These inlets are not for the marginally experienced.

The coast along this part of the New Jersey shore stretches south-southwest in a nearly straight line from Manasquan to the next inlet, Barnegat Inlet, 25 miles to the south. Nearly all inlets along the New Jersey coast are characterized by shoals near the mouth of the inlet that extend well offshore. Over the last few centuries these shoals have accounted for innumerable shipwrecks. Frequently, when time is not a constraint, we enjoy traveling along the coast, close to shore. It enables us to see the sights and can give protection from the wind and waves if the wind is coming from onshore. But I always remember, when approaching inlets, to check the chart and to move out well beyond the shoals. When time is of the essence or when we are traveling in fog, we stay well offshore on rhumb-line courses that provide the shortest route and keep us well to seaward of the inlet shoals, but also out of the shipping lanes. An example of this would be the trip between Atlantic City and the sea buoy off Wildwood, which is considerably shorter and safer than following the coast.

Wind conditions should seriously be considered when electing to begin the offshore passage along New Jersey's coast. When the wind is from the west, even if very strong, the waves in the ocean close to the coast are small. Strong winds from the northeast, east, or southeast are another matter and should be evaluated before one commits to the offshore passage. Since wave heights are proportional to the wind speed and the *fetch* of these winds, that is, the distance the wind has had to form them, a prolonged wind blowing in from the ocean can make things a bit lumpy.

One of the most positive things we've noticed during our trips in the last few years is the dramatic increase in water quality as we cruise along the shoreline. Last year, when we looked down into the water near shore, we were reminded of being in the Caribbean, and each year we encounter more schools of dolphins and whales traveling along the coast.

As we begin our offshore passage south from Manasquan, the Ferris wheel and roller-coaster will be the first distinctive landmarks that identify Seaside. Just below Seaside, development on the shore ends as we come abreast of Island Beach State Park. By now, on a clear day we'll be able to see the red top of the Barnegat Lighthouse to the south, raising its head above the sand dunes of Island Beach and providing an unmistakable fix.

Barnegat Lighthouse, 161 feet high, red on its upper half and white on its lower half, is listed on the charts as abandoned. It is no longer navigational, and only shows a token light. For purposes of coastal navigation at night, the location of Barnegat Inlet is easily seen by the demarcation line between the dark shores of Island Beach State Park and the lights of Long Beach Island, making the lighthouse superfluous. Barnegat Inlet is protected by jetties on the north and south. The jetties have towers on their outer ends. There is a Coast Guard station near the lighthouse, in the town of Barnegat Light, just inside Barnegat Inlet. It can be reached on VHF Ch-16 or Ch-22A.

Those unfamiliar with Barnegat Inlet should *only* use it under ideal sea conditions, preferably on a rising tide and, if possible, while watching and following one of the local commercial fishing boats into the entrance channel. This is a prudent approach, since the location of the entrance bars and of deep water changes with every storm. As with all New Jersey inlets, tides sweep in and out from the Atlantic Ocean with two high and two low every day, so that the bottom contours, as well as the shoreline, is in a constant state of change. One should be aware when approaching Barnegat Inlet that the northern breakwater may be submerged at high tide and will not show up on the radar. Taking a shortcut between the outer tower and the shore means going on the rocks. When there are breakers across the entrance bar, the rule is: don't use the inlet; at the very least, a call to the Coast Guard is recommended. Whenever I use Barnegat Inlet, even though I've used it all my life, everyone aboard dons life jackets—it's a given. It's not unusual for several people to die here nearly every year.

Donna and Robert McGowan went fishing inside Barnegat Inlet in their 20-foot Grady-White on a beautiful, calm, spring day. Donna recalls: "It was about 9:30 in the morning, and we were fishing in the inlet, well inside the breakwaters. There had been a storm earlier in the week, but the sea conditions were now relatively calm. Suddenly I glanced over my shoulder and saw this large wave coming through the inlet. It began to break just as it came to us and sucked our boat up into the curl and flipped it over. I seemed to be under water for a very long time, but finally we both surfaced. Our boat was a total loss, but the Coast Guard said we were one of the lucky few that had survived a capsize within the Inlet."

The name Barnegat is a corruption of the original Dutch description "Barende-gat," or "Breakers Inlet," and it is appropriately named, since breakers across the entrance can occur even on relatively calm days. As with most inlets, going out is always easier than returning. Once, when going out, I powered into the curl of a huge breaker, which broke on the foredeck and cabin top, soaking me from head to foot and nearly filling the cockpit. Another time I received a real scare. As I was entering the inlet, the wave I was riding began to break, and I surfed all the way through the inlet at high speed on the face of the breaker between the stone jetties. I repeated to myself, "Don't broach! Don't broach!" all the way in.

Aerial view of Barnegat Inlet. To the north of the inlet is the undeveloped Island Beach State Park, and to the south the resort island of Long Beach Island. Note the change of direction of the shoreline at Barnegat Inlet and the typical shoals that extend well offshore (photo courtesy of Keith Hamilton, Studio-9, Waretown)

Chart 7.1 Barnegat Inlet (reproduced from NOAA's Chart #12324)

In 1991, a multimillion dollar south jetty project was completed in the hope of deepening and stabilizing Barnegat Inlet. Although it has seemed to help, it is too soon to tell whether the anticipated results will permanently stabilize the inlet. One thing that is certain is the tidal currents within the inlet have increased considerably, and at the height of the tide change underpowered auxiliaries will have a hard time bucking the opposing current. This increased tidal flow, caused by the recent changes, may have been an important contributing factor in the Barnegat Bay flood tides of Halloween 1991 and in the December nor'easter of 1992.

As we pass Barnegat Inlet the coastline takes a turn to the southwest and continues in that direction all the way to Cape May (chart 7.1). Sailors who have been close-hauled to the prevailing southwest winds up to now may find they have to fire up the iron wind or else tack down the coast.

The next inlet south of Barnegat is 22 miles away, at the end of Long Beach Island.

This island was the site of an unusual encounter during the War of 1812. The USS *Constitution* (*Old Ironsides,* which is now berthed in Boston Harbor) was sailing up the New Jersey coast from the Chesapeake, destined for New York Harbor. At twilight on July 17, 1813, in the failing light, Captain Isaac Hull sighted sails and believed them to be the American ships with which he had a rendezvous. The wind was dying, and he dropped anchor near the south end of Long Beach Island so that the *Constitution* would not drift ashore.

At first light the next morning, with the fog beginning to lift, Hull discovered he was anchored near a British flotilla that consisted of five ships carrying 172 cannon. He had no U.S. flag flying, so he decided to steal away in spite of the glassy, calm sea surface and the absence of wind; he launched the ship's boats, silently raised anchor, and towed the *Constitution* away from the British fleet.

It wasn't long before the British discovered what was happening and opened up with broadsides from all of the ships' guns, but by now the *Constitution* was out of range. Captain Hull ordered the American flag hoisted and returned fire from his stern cannons, and although he too was out of range, the cannonade helped propel the ship forward.

Then, in an effort to put even more room between themselves and the British, the American crew began kedging, by rowing small anchors out ahead in the longboats and hauling up to them from the deck of the ship. Soon the British began doing the same. This labor continued on the unusually still sea for three days. The *Constitution* and the British flotilla pulled themselves up the coast, past Barnegat Inlet and Island Beach until a squall allowed the *Constitution* to hoist sail and escape.

As we make our way south, along the tortuous route taken by the *Constitution,* we near the southern end of Long Beach Island; the last 2 miles at the south end of the island are undeveloped and have been set aside as a wildlife refuge.

Just beyond the refuge are the twin inlets of Beach Haven and Little Egg. Because of the numerous wrecks and shoals and the changing channel, Beach Haven Inlet to the north has been officially closed to navigation by the Coast Guard; the inlet is unmarked. It appears that it is on its way to becoming dry land and a part of Long Beach Island. If one has to use an inlet in this area, Little Egg Inlet is the only viable one, close to the south of the old Beach Haven Inlet. It is well buoyed but, as with most inlets along the coast, these buoys are uncharted due to the constantly shifting shoals. When using Little Egg Inlet keep a sharp eye out for any dog-leg turns in this 2-mile-long entrance channel. They can easily be overlooked.

In heavy weather Little Egg Inlet should also be avoided by the inexperienced, since breakers can form all the way across the bar and are frequently on the beam when the wind is from the northeast.

Two and a half miles down the coast from Little Egg Inlet is Brigantine In-

Aerial view of the southern tip of Long Beach Island and the twin inlets of Beach Haven and Little Egg (photo courtesy of Keith Hamilton, Studio-9, Waretown)

Aerial view of Atlantic City. Note the large expanses of wetlands west of the city through which the ICW meanders (photo courtesy of Keith Hamilton, Studio-9, Waretown)

let, which has shoaled-in to such an extent that even the smallest of boats with local knowledge consider it unsafe. Cross this one off your list.

Nearly 10 miles below Little Egg Inlet is Absecon Inlet, one of the best on the coast. The high rises and casinos make it obvious that this is Atlantic City, which is on Absecon Island. It is home to a large fleet of commercial fishing boats as well as recreational craft. The inlet is frequently used by transients who use Atlantic City as either a destination or stopover point on their offshore trip north or south along the coast.

The great granite rocks of the north and south jetties are far apart, making this inlet the broadest of New Jersey's improved inlets. Don't come too close to the shore when approaching from the north; a shoal extends well to seaward of the north jetty and has been responsible for many groundings.

When a break in the offshore passage from Manasquan to Cape May is planned, or if the weather is becoming marginal and the seas are beginning to kick up, the Absecon Inlet at Atlantic City is the inlet to use for an overnight berth, a refuge, a chance for a meal ashore, some sightseeing, or a try at the gambling tables. (For more information on Atlantic City marinas and facilities, see chapter 5.)

The 167-foot tall Absecon Lighthouse at Atlantic City, like Barnegat Lighthouse, is now listed as abandoned and is even difficult to locate from offshore, having been obscured by the surrounding high rises and casinos. When it was constructed in 1856, it was 1,300 feet from water's edge, but within twenty

Atlantic City as seen from the ocean

The Absecon Lighthouse at Atlantic City

years the shore had eroded to within 75 feet of the structure. The light was in operation until 1932, when it was decommissioned and deeded to the state. After World War II it was scheduled for demolition, but public outcry saved it. (Both the Absecon Lighthouse and the Barnegat Lighthouse were designed by George Meade, who was also the Union commander at the battle of Gettysburg.) The Absecon Lighthouse is painted in distinctive colors, as are all lighthouses, to differentiate it from any other; in this case, it is white with a red band at the center.

Ventnor, Atlantic City's nearest neighbor to the south, would have been part of the city, but a narrow inlet existed between them in the 1880s, when the railroad came through and the building boom started. As the years passed, this inlet began slowly filling in and was finally dubbed Dry Inlet. It is now Jackson Avenue.

Eight miles south of Absecon Inlet, at the south end of Absecon Island, is Great Egg Harbor Inlet, which enters through the barrier islands just north of Ocean City (chart 7.2). The Ferris wheel at Ocean City makes it easily identifiable from offshore. Ocean City's Great Egg Harbor Inlet is reasonably safe in calm to moderate conditions but is subject to continual change and shoaling. The uncharted entrance buoys are frequently shifted to mark the best water, as storms continually rearrange the bottom. The inlet is used mainly by local

Great Egg Harbor Inlet, Ocean City

Chart 7.2 Great Egg Harbor Inlet and Ocean City (reproduced from NOAA's Chart #12316)

boats, but a visit there is well worth it, and there are several large marina complexes that welcome transients.

When planning to stay at Ocean City for a day or more, be sure to visit Ocean City's beach, which is superb. The Great Egg Coast Guard Station is in a small basin just south of the bridge. It can be reached on Ch-16 or Ch-22A.

Often, when looking at charts of this area, people wonder why Great Egg Harbor is smaller than Little Egg Harbor, which is located further to the north. The answer lies in the size of the eggs rather than the size of the bays. The early explorers, when pilfering eggs from the nests of sea birds, discovered the eggs were bigger on the smaller harbor to the south.

Twenty miles south of Atlantic City, and just to the north of Avalon, one comes to Townsends Inlet. As with all of New Jersey's so-called unimproved inlets, entrance buoys are not charted. The bascule bridge directly across Townsends Inlet has a closed clearance of 23 feet and the ICW is just inside the bridge. Shoaling has been reported under the bridge that can create swirling currents during tide changes. From off the shore of Avalon, on a clear day, one can see the high rises of Atlantic City in the distance.

Several years ago, when sailing along this section of the coastline, we had our first and only encounter with a *microburst*. The microburst, a recently recognized meteorological phenomenon, is a blast of hurricane-force wind that only lasts a few seconds and is out of proportion to the prevailing wind conditions. They occur when cloud conditions are just right, creating an intense downdraft. They are frequently associated with thunderstorms but have been known to occur even in apparently fine weather. Old-time sailors called them "white squalls." Microbursts have been the cause of plane crashes and they have sent many ships and small boats to the bottom. The phenomenon has been cited as the probable cause for the sinking of *The Pride of Baltimore* and of the *Cutty Sark* replica, as well as many other substantial and well-built boats, both power and sail.

When we had our microburst experience, Elsie and I were sailing close to the shore, with every stitch of sail flying—the wind all day had not exceeded 10 knots. Suddenly, and without warning, we were struck by a blast of a 60 to 70 mile-an-hour wind for five or ten seconds. Our boat is "stiff"; it is hard to get the rail wet on the windiest of days, but the boat was immediately laid over, and we had solid water on the deck. Although I was afraid the water might go into the open portholes, the wind was back to 10 knots before I was able to roundup and was gentle for the rest of the day.

If you hug the shoreline when traveling south, as we were doing that day, you'll notice that the coastline at Avalon juts out about a mile farther than the coastline to the north. Shoaling extends for three-quarters of a mile beyond that so, if you are traveling close to shore, a detour well offshore is mandatory.

Twenty-eight miles south from Atlantic City, and just north of Wildwood, you'll come to Hereford Inlet. Due to the constantly changing shoals and breakers that are present there at all times, strangers should not attempt the passage. The shoal waters at the mouth of the inlet extend a good mile off-shore, and at low tide there is a sandbar awash, locally known as "Champagne Island."

The historic and attractive Hereford Inlet Lighthouse, which is only 46 feet high, is hard to find from offshore. It went into service in 1874 and, after a severe 1913 storm, it was undermined and finally relocated 150 feet west. This unusual Victorian-style lighthouse, which is open to the public, is in a two-story building that is topped by the light tower. It was taken over by the city of North Wildwood in 1982, and its restoration has been undertaken by a group of local citizens, members of the Hereford Inlet Lighthouse Commission.

If a visit to the Wildwoods is on the schedule they can be reached more safely by entering Cape May Inlet further south and then taking the Intracoastal Waterway north. Bridges on this short inland passage between Cape May Inlet and the Wildwoods are bascule, so even sailboats can make the trip.

Wildwood

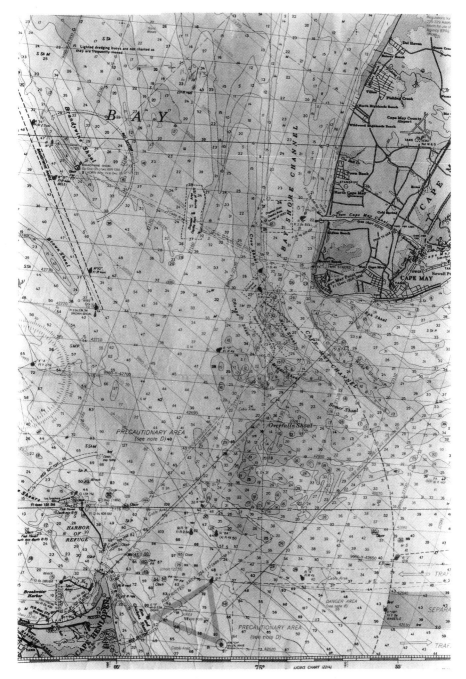

$\mathcal{C}$hart 7.3 The mouth of Delaware Bay between Cape May and Cape
Henlopen (reproduced from NOAA's Chart #12304)

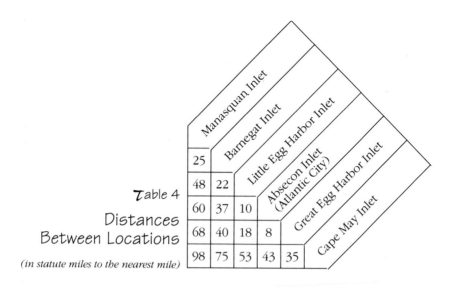

Table 4

Distances
Between Locations

(in statute miles to the nearest mile)

	Manasquan Inlet	Barnegat Inlet	Little Egg Harbor Inlet	Absecon Inlet (Atlantic City)	Great Egg Harbor Inlet	Cape May Inlet
	25					
	48	22				
	60	37	10			
	68	40	18	8		
	98	75	53	43	35	

Cape May inlet was formerly listed on the charts by its original name, Cold Spring Harbor Inlet; but, since nobody ever called it that, NOAA has finally dropped the appellation and it is now shown on the charts as Cape May Inlet. This deep, nearly all-weather inlet is enclosed by breakwaters and leads into the harbor of Cape May, where marinas, stores, and restaurants abound within walking or biking distance. Just inside the Cape May Inlet, the New Jersey Intracoastal Waterway system comes to an end, where the Cape May Inlet, the Cape May Harbor, and the ICW merge. A trip west down Cape May's harbor brings us to the Cape May Canal, which gives access to Delaware Bay for boats that are able to pass under the two fixed bridges (55-foot clearance at high tide).

Skippers of boats with masts over 55 feet, and those who elect to remain offshore and enter Delaware Bay from the ocean, should approach the shallow waters at the tip of Cape May with caution. The joining of the Delaware Bay and the Atlantic is strewn with shoals: Prissy Wicks, Overfalls, McCrie, Five Fathom Bank, and others (chart 7.3). If one has local knowledge, a transit around the tip of the cape can be made a few hundred yards offshore. Note that on either side of this passage, depths at low tide can be 2 feet. A stranger to the area would be safer entering Cape May Channel from about 4 miles offshore, around the eastern end of Prissy Wicks Shoal.

Of the various entrances from the ocean into Delaware Bay, the most conservative approach is probably by way of the large-ship channel just to the north of Cape Henlopen, Delaware. The ocean sands along this southern tip of New Jersey are constantly shifting, and the buoys are frequently uncharted because of their constant relocation. Even the charted buoys may not be where they are expected.

Whether by the intracoastal route or by the offshore route, we have now reached New Jersey's southeastern corner, Cape May, where we will stop over before cruising New Jersey's south coast, the Delaware Bay.

In the next chapter we'll explore Delaware Bay and its tributaries, from Cape May to the mouth of the Delaware River, at the juncture of the Chesapeake and Delaware Canal.

Chapter Eight

Delaware Bay and Its Tributaries

$\mathcal{O}$f all the navigable tidewater along the east coast, Delaware Bay is probably the least known and least loved. It is one of the few places along the Atlantic coast where skippers can find themselves completely alone and, at times, out of sight of land, even though on inland waters. The 50-mile, nearly straight line up the bay from the Cape May Canal to the Chesapeake and Delaware Canal (hereafter referred to as the C&D), is considered a chore by many, to be quickly navigated. The uninhabited shore can appear bleak and generally devoid of scenic variety. The green and brown expanse of low marshlands possesses few towns, marinas, or other signs of life, except for migratory birds overhead, muskrats on shore, and a few fishermen, crabbers, or oysterers off the channel. In the main channel yachts must share the water with giant commercial ships that serve the industrial ports on the Delaware River and on the northern Chesapeake Bay.

Normal tide ranges of about 5 to 6 feet create a one to two knot tidal flow, and seas in these relatively shallow waters can build into a steep, short chop, with buoys out of sight even in clear weather, and few obvious places of refuge.

Most skippers crossing the bay pick up a feeling of emptiness and loneliness. No wonder they want to complete the trip across the bay as soon as possible. To others, though, the bay provides a sense of tranquility and solitude. It may be one of the few stretches of New Jersey's inland waters where the cruising skipper can experience the solitary existence of the offshore sailor and feel charged with a lone responsibility and independence not felt along the populated shores that make up the rest of the state's coastline. Skippers who are confident of their skills and willing to test them find the bay interesting to explore and its very remoteness a balm to the soul. The sparse landscape invites reflection.

⚓ ⚓

Instead of a featureless shoreline, the interested boater sees marshlands teeming with life. The yellow grass, *Spartina patens,* also called salt grass, along the shoreline, is a sanctuary to millions of migratory birds, whose flight paths range from Argentina to the Canadian tundra. On the bay, oysterers are at work trying to restore their once prolific industry, and fishermen fish the bay or use it as access to Atlantic waters. On our last trip, near the mouth of the bay, we sighted a pilot whale and on nearly every cruise in recent years we have been joined by dolphin, evidence that the bay's long history of pollution may finally be reversing.

The eastern end of the bay joins the Atlantic between Cape May, New Jersey, to the north, and Cape Henlopen, Delaware, on the south. The waters here can be, alternately, a formidable foe or a calm and tranquil friend.

The waters and shores of Delaware Bay have experienced only limited changes since their discovery by European explorers. In the early 1600s, about the same time the *Mayflower* landed at Cape Cod, Dutch explorer Cornelius Mey, traversing the coast in his ship *Fortune,* modestly named the two capes after himself. The southern cape became Cape Cornelius and the northern cape, Cape Mey. "Hindelopen," also named in honor of a Dutch mariner, designated the area south of Cape Cornelius. This name, becoming Henlopen, was finally used to designate the entire area of the southern cape while, with a slight spelling change, May came to designate the northern cape.

Well before the Dutch, Swedish, and English explorers traveled through the area, Native Americans paddled across the 17 miles of sea between the tips of the two capes in their flimsy canoes.

In modern times, the trip has been made easier with a ferry service between the capes, but not until 1964, after lengthy negotiations between authorities from New Jersey and Delaware. The Cape May–Lewes Ferry, which travels between Cape May and Lewes (pronounced Lewis), Delaware, provides access to the Delmarva peninsula for those heading south by car, by bike, or on foot, and to Atlantic City gambling facilities for ferry customers heading north from such places as Delaware, Maryland, and Virginia.

As with nearly all the estuaries along the Atlantic Coast, Delaware Bay and the Delaware River have always been strategically important during wartime, from as far back as the Revolution. During the War of 1812, the British blockaded the mouth of the Delaware River in an effort to close down the Port of Philadelphia and, during the First World War, Delaware Bay was also a site of conflict. In May of 1918, the German submarine U-151, very low on supplies, entered Delaware Bay. Because of the shallow bay waters the submarine operated on the surface. It intercepted three schooners, confiscated their food and supplies, and took all three twenty-six-member crews prisoner. TNT

The Cape May–Lewes Ferry

charges were placed on board the schooners and ignited, sending the ships to the bottom of the bay. The U-151 crew members then laid mines across the mouth of the bay and sank thirteen more ships in the waters off New Jersey and New York before heading back to Germany.

Today, as we head across Delaware Bay in our schooner, the waters look so tranquil that it's hard to believe they were the scene of such conflict.

Small boats that leave Cape May Harbor, destined for the Delaware Bay crossing, have easy access to the bay via the Cape May Canal; it starts at the southwestern tip of Cape May Harbor and cuts across the southern end of the cape to Delaware Bay (chart 8.1). Unfortunately, very large sailboats will be prevented from using this route by the two 55-foot fixed bridges crossing the canal. The only alternative is to go out through the Cape May Inlet and enter Delaware Bay from the ocean.

For the majority of boats, the Cape May Canal is the easiest answer. Tidal flow in the canal seldom reaches two and a half knots, which is generally not a problem on this short run. Be sure to observe the six knot speed limit in the canal, which prevents excessive erosion along the nonbulkheaded banks.

Halfway down the canal, just before the second fixed highway bridge, we encounter a railroad swing bridge. For years this rail link had been unused and the bridge had rusted into the open position, but a few years ago this spur of

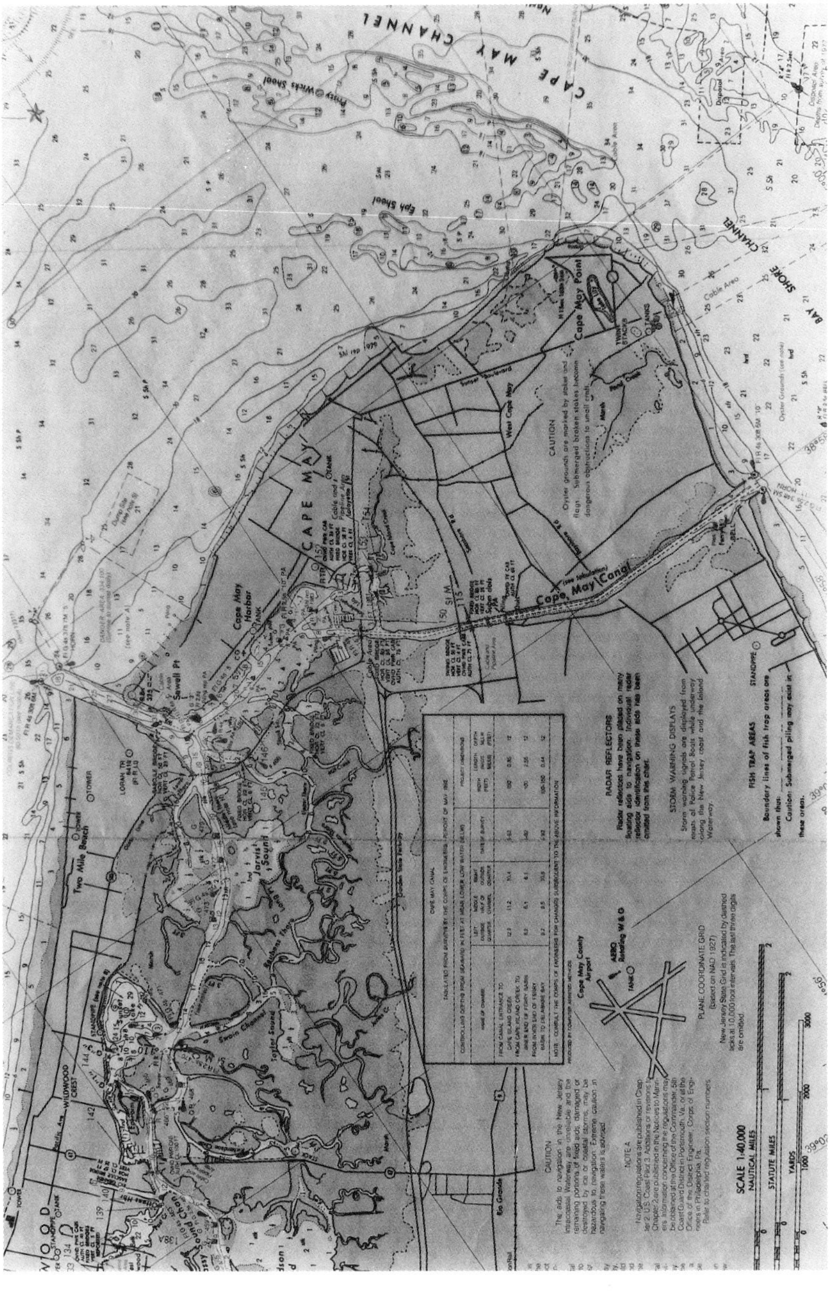

Chart 8.1 Cape May Inlet, Harbor, and Canal (reproduced from NOAA's Chart #12316)

The Cape May Canal

the railroad was reactivated. The bridge received extensive repairs and was put back into service. It is normally left in the open position unless there is rail traffic, and then it only closes for about ten minutes, which is not a great hardship for those using the canal.

At the western end of the canal, just before emerging into Delaware Bay, we pass the terminal for the Cape May–Lewes Ferry. If a ferry is seen either leaving or arriving, it would be wise to wait for it to clear. Ferries create large wakes between the entrance breakwaters and also turbulence in the canal; when turning, a ferry takes up the whole waterway.

Before starting a trip across Delaware Bay, we always check the VHF weather channel so we'll know what to expect. The Delaware Bay can change its personality within an hour. Northwest and southwest winds, along the axis of the bay, can cause a high, short chop, and gale winds from either of these directions can build seas to 10 feet or more near the mouth of the bay. During the summer months the prevailing southerly winds are reinforced by a sea breeze and seas tend to build as the day progresses. Visibility is generally good, but during the spring and early summer (April, May, and June), advection fog is common, reducing visibility to a boat length. These fogs often lift as

The Cape May–Lewes Ferry terminal near the western end of the Cape May Canal

The Delaware Bay entrance to the Cape May Canal

the day progresses, especially close to shore. Fog is much less likely to be encountered during July, August, and September.

Once within the bay proper, water depth, at least for the recreational boat, is not a major concern. But, there are numerous shoals at the entrance to the bay. These created problems as far back as 1609, when Henry Hudson was looking for the Northwest Passage. He entered Delaware Bay in his 80-ton ship, *The Half Moon,* and promptly ran aground on one of these shoals. In the ship's log Hudson wrote: "He that will thoroughly discover this great bay must have a small Pinnace, that must draw but four or five feet of water, to sound before him."

Most small boats that traverse the bay between Cape May and the C&D canals avoid the main channel where the large ships navigate. This channel is 1,000 feet wide in the bay and 400 feet wide in the Delaware River, leading to Philadelphia and Camden. There is plenty of water for small craft outside this channel, so boats can avoid competing with heavy shipping. A nearly straight-line course from the Cape May Canal to Ship John Shoal Lighthouse avoids travel in the roughest waters of the bay; it is locally called "going across the flats." This rhumb-line course between the Cape May Canal and Ship John Shoal Lighthouse, which is situated just south of the Cohansey River, is 317 degrees true, and will take recreational craft well away from Brandywine Shoal.

This straight-line route across the bay will also bypass Cross Ledge shoal, where the ruins of an abandoned lighthouse can be seen on its southeastern edge. Cross Ledge shoal is west of Egg Island Point and just east of the main channel.

Along this route skippers will encounter some recreational and commercial fishing boats and crab-pot buoys, as well as frequent vertical PVC pipes that mark oyster beds.

Although the direct route from the Cape May Canal to Ship John Shoal Lighthouse is the only part of Delaware Bay seen by most transient boaters, there are many other interesting options.

When leaving the Cape May Canal, if one heads north instead of heading for the Delaware River, the route will lead to the Maurice (pronounced Morris) River (chart 8.2). In the 1630s a Dutch ship, *The Maurice,* named for the Prince of Orange-Nassau in the Netherlands, was captured by Indians and burned near the mouth of this river, giving the river its name.

The Maurice River was also the center of activity for Delaware Bay's oyster fleet from the early 1700s until 1957, when a parasitic blight destroyed most of the oyster beds in Delaware Bay. Prior to the 1957 blight, Delaware Bay was the source of oysters for most of the major East Coast cities; but almost overnight the rich oyster beds suffered such damage that they were nearly

A restored World War-II PT boat on Delaware Bay

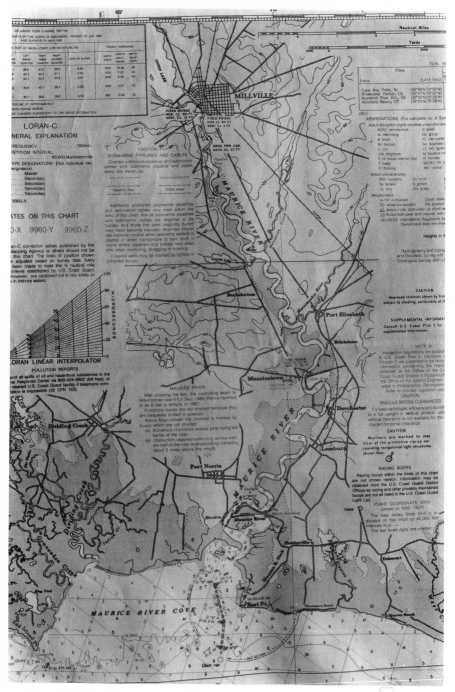

$\mathcal{C}$hart 8.2 The Maurice River (reproduced from NOAA's Chart #12304)

annihilated. The appropriately named towns of Bivalve and Shellpile, on the Maurice River, were once home to between five and six hundred oyster schooners and other sailing vessels, and oysters were shipped to distributors throughout the northeast from Bivalve's railroad terminal. A half-century after the oyster blight, the industry in the bay is still trying to make a comeback.

Rutgers University researchers are currently working at the Haskin Shellfish Research Lab in Port Norris, located on the Maurice River (under grants from the U.S. Commerce Department), seeking to develop a disease-resistant hybrid of American and Pacific oysters. The hybrid must be resistant to the two oyster-killing parasites, Dermo and MSX (neither of which is harmful to humans), which were responsible for the 1957 devastation.

In December 1993, President Clinton designated 37 miles of the Maurice River and three of its tributaries—the Mushee, Menantico, and Manumuskin creeks—as part of the National Wild and Historic Scenic Rivers System. The legal implication of this designation is to preserve the waterway and to regulate future development along its banks. In recent years ospreys have returned to the Maurice River, nearly a dozen families, as well as more than sixteen bald eagles, which hunt up and down the river.

A trip up the Maurice River makes for a wonderful excursion, The river is well buoyed and there are several marinas along the way. The head of navigation on the Maurice River is at Millville, where the 898-acre Lake Union empties into the river over a dam, making this the limit of navigation. The lake that was created by the dam backs the water up for almost 4 miles. South of the lake the river is tidal, while on the river north of the lake, the waters are a canoeing and kayaking delight (see *Exploring the Little Rivers of New Jersey* by Cawley and Cawley, Rutgers University Press, 1993).

When heading for the Maurice River, look for the red-roofed East Point Lighthouse on the east side of the entrance; it's a daytime marker that can be seen far down the bay. Built in 1849 on a jut of land once known as Dead Man's Shoal, its purpose was to keep ships from grounding at this point as well as to provide a navigational landmark identifying the entrance into the Maurice River. The lighthouse was in operation until 1941. The two and a half story brick structure has a cupola on top where the beacon was housed; it is now owned by the Maurice River Historical Society which has restored it from its previous state of disrepair.

Buoys mark the channel entrance to the Maurice. Here, as with most of New Jersey's tidewaters, strong winds can change water depths considerably. This holds true for other streams off Delaware Bay, where blow-in and blow-out tides can affect water depth across the entrance bars. The marked channel into the Maurice River passes east of Fowler Island, which is in the middle of the river's mouth. Beyond the entrance bar, the river runs very deep through flat marshlands. Visitors can anchor behind the island, at the mouth of the river, or farther up the river, off the channel. When anchoring, allow for the 6-foot tide and a rapid tidal flow.

Several years ago, in Port Norris, a reclamation project was started to restore the old oyster schooner *A. J. Meerwald*. The 115-foot-long schooner, was originally built in 1928 as a Delaware Bay oyster dredge for the Meerwald family of Cape May County. In 1942, during World War II, she was pressed into service as a fire boat by the Coast Guard and returned to the Meerwald family after the war, in 1947. She was sold to Clyde A. Phipps later that year. When the oyster blight struck the bay, ownership passed to Cornelius Campbell, and in 1989 she was donated to the Schooner Project (now known as the Bayshore Discovery Project). Now, through an extensive restoration effort, the *A. J. Meerwald* tours the state as a floating classroom. The thousands of passengers each year who visit the schooner are provided with on-board educational programs relating to the history, culture, and ecology of the Delaware Bay estuary, as well as other waters around the state.

The Bayshore Discovery Project also sponsors public, private, and educational sailings aboard the tall ship; educational and exploratory learning programs; the Delaware Bay Museum in Port Norris; a schooner day-camp, and many other events on land and water, under the watchful eyes of professional seamen and a host of knowledgeable volunteers. For more information go to: www.ajmeerwald.org.

In 1995 the *A. J. Meerwald* was added to the National Register of Historic Places and was designated as New Jersey's official "Tall Ship" by Governor Christine Whitman in 1998.

North of Port Norris the river continues to snake through wetlands on its lower reaches, but as we approach Millville, 20 miles upriver, the banks become higher and more settled.

Both the New Jersey and Delaware shorelines of Delaware Bay are marshlands, so remember, when either anchored out or in a marina during the summer months, screening is vital. What these shores lack in flora is more than made up in tiny fauna. The greenhead fly, which inhabits the coastal marshlands from Georgia north, can be troublesome during the day; mosquitoes become bothersome around sunset, and on windless days, no-see-ums can be annoying.

As one heads west from the Maurice River along the marshlands on the northern shoreline of the bay, Egg Island Point provides a good landmark. West of the point, the harbor town of Fortescue is home to a large fishing fleet. Empty slips for transients are nearly nonexistent here during the height of the

This 1994 photograph shows the A. J. Meerwald restoration project under way on the banks of the Maurice River

The A. J. Meerwald, now New Jersey's official "Tall Ship" sailing the waters of the Delaware Bay (photo courtesy of George Schupp, Bayshore Discovery Project volunteer)

season. The entrance into the harbor at Fortescue has about 4 feet at low water and there is a sharp turn just inside the mouth. During the summer months the Coast Guard operates a search-and-rescue team out of Fortescue.

Along the shore, about 6 miles northwest of Fortescue, the 30-foot tower, with a six-second flashing light at Ben Davis point, marks the entrance to Back Creek, which can be used as a storm shelter. There are no facilities here, but the creek has navigable water for about 2 miles upstream.

When we find the weather rapidly deteriorating, or when a shower and a meal ashore are in order, we frequently take a detour into the Cohansey River, whose entrance is located about 2 nautical miles north of Ship John Shoal Lighthouse. The lighthouse, one of the oldest on the bay, is located about midway between the Cape May and C&D canals. Ship John Shoal Lighthouse is surrounded by riprap and is easily visible for miles. (The lighthouse was built on the shoal where the ship *John* went aground in December of 1797.)

The Cohansey is by far the most convenient and safest harbor of refuge for boats traveling between the two canals, since it is not far off the main channel; but the tower on the entrance island, at the mouth of the Cohansey, can be easily confused with several other towers along this section of shoreline. A Loran or GPS fix can confirm the entrance, which is about a quarter of a mile northwest from the skeletal entrance tower.

The Ship John Shoal Lighthouse

Although the entrance into the river can be made on either side of the entrance island, the buoyed dredged cut northwest of the island, on which the tower stands, is preferred. We leave the unmarked entrance on the other side of the island to the locals.

Once inside the entrance, one will find that this deep stream meanders with indecision through the meadowlands, it is navigable all the way to Bridgeton, the seat of Cumberland County.

About 3 miles up from the mouth of the river there are two marinas situated a few hundred yards apart. Both usually have space available for transients and deep water at dockside. The first marina, Hancock's Harbor, offers gas, diesel, and a few supplies, as well as showers and a home-style restaurant that is popular with locals. The restaurant is closed on Monday and Tuesday. After a rough day on the bay it is a refreshing place to stop, clean up, and get away from the galley.

The second marina, Ship John Inn and Marina, has dockage for transients, diesel, gas, showers, washers and dryers, a travel lift, and it is capable of providing major repair services. It has a marine store that stocks a large variety of engine parts and marine supplies, which can usually provide for most of our basic on-board needs. The Ship John Inn, adjacent to the marina, offers cocktails, supper and, frequently, live entertainment. It, too, is closed Monday and Tuesday.

The nearby residential town of Greenwich (pronounced "green-which"), about a mile from the northern Ship John Marina, was the scene of New Jersey's version of the Boston Tea Party in December 1774 (a year after the event in Boston). In Greenwich, the tea was off-loaded from the brig *Greyhound,* which was anchored in the Cohansey. It was seized by protesters, who were dressed as American Indians, and burned in an open field.

From the Ship John Marina, the 1 mile walk or bike ride into the town of Greenwich takes one up Pier Road to a right turn on Market Street, and then a left turn on Ye Greate Street. The Greenwich General Store and Historical Society will be found to the right, and a little further along on the left, one will come to the Maritime Museum. The general store has nearly everything one needs for restocking the galley, and the town's post office is located in the same building.

If we decide on anchoring out for the night on the Cohansey, we usually anchor off the channel near one of the bends in the river. Anchoring in this deep river requires lots of anchor rode, since inside the entrance bar the river runs very deep. Recently, to escape gale winds and heavy seas on the bay, we anchored just beyond the first bend in the river. We had 200 feet of anchor line out and still couldn't get a 6:1 scope.

Chart 8.3 The Cohansey River (reproduced from NOAA's Chart #12304)

The Hancock Harbor Marina on the Cohansey River near Greenwich

Our schooner, *Delphinus*, at the Ship John Marina

When anchoring in any of the rivers off Delaware Bay or when approaching a dock at one of the marinas, be aware that there is a nominal 6-foot tide. At the heights of tide changes, the water doesn't saunter—it races. Before approaching a dock, first determine the tidal flow and then make the approach into the flow for maximum control. Floating docks are the norm, helping to keep fenders properly positioned. When a planned departure time for the next day is fixed, it is a good idea to calculate tide flow beforehand. If it will be coming from astern, and if it appears there might be problems when leaving the dock, we turn our boat around at the next convenient slack water and sleep better that night. This precaution can be especially important for auxiliaries, whose power is limited and whose underwater configuration is more readily affected by the tidal flow—and I speak from experience.

When leaving the Cohansey and heading up the bay, be sure to go around the end of Dunks Bar. As one travels farther up the bay, the shorelines of Delaware and New Jersey are closer together, as Delaware Bay becomes Delaware River.

The demarcation line between bay and river wasn't established until 1905, when the New Jersey and Delaware legislatures created a commission to draw the line. This arbitrary and imaginary line, 42 miles above the Delaware capes,

The nuclear plants on Artificial Island

runs between the southern entrance to Hope Creek, New Jersey, and Liston point, Delaware. Stone markers on both shores make it official. In spite of the official demarcation line, boaters usually consider the bay to be between the C&D and Cape May canals.

Farther up the bay, the twin domes of the Salem Nuclear Plant on Artificial Island are shown on government charts; the plant's huge cooling tower, with water vapor emanating from the top, dominates the landscape. This type of tower is used to cool the water from the turbine generators, and engineers call this strange shape a hyperbolic cooling tower, after the geometric curves used in its design. This nuclear facility is operated by Public Service Electric and Gas Company. The two domes shown on the chart are separate nuclear reactors, Salem-1 and Salem-2. These reactors, built by Westinghouse and plagued with problems in recent years, began service in 1977. When operating properly, they can supply more than 2 billion watts of electricity, enough for 2 million homes. The third dome is that of the newer Hope Creek Nuclear Plant, built by G.E. It's just a few hundred feet from the Salem plant domes. The Hope Creek Nuclear Plant, which went into service in 1987, is a stellar performer that receives little publicity.

Between Artificial Island—the location of the nuclear plants—and the channel, there is a designated anchorage area for commercial craft and barges. Located in this anchorage are black, steel anchor buoys, which are nearly submerged and easily missed—especially when the tide is running, in twilight hours, in a rough chop, or in fog. If you plan a shortcut through this anchorage, keep a sharp lookout.

Magnetic variations of up to 5 degrees have been noted on this part of the river, from Artificial Island all the way up the river to Marcus Hook, Pennsylvania, and these have existed long before the nuclear age. At the north end of Artificial Island, the boundary agreement between New Jersey and Delaware specifies that the river between this point and the Pennsylvania state line is entirely within the state of Delaware, the boundary between the two states being the high-tide mark on the New Jersey shoreline.

North of Artificial Island on the west shore of the Delaware River is the entrance to the Chesapeake and Delaware Canal, the C&D, which joins the Delaware River with the north end of Chesapeake Bay.

On the other side of the river from the C&D, one will find two marinas on the Salem River. They are the distance of a long walk, a bike trip, or a cab ride from the town of Salem. (The old town of Salem, settled by the Quakers in 1675, has a rich history.)

The entrance to the Salem River is by way of the buoyed channel markers running north-northeast. No shortcuts here! Shoal water is on both sides of the

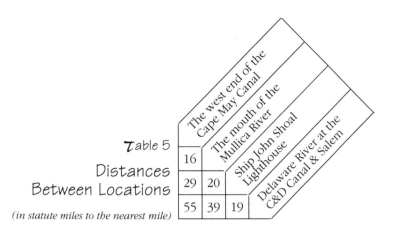

Table 5

Distances
Between Locations

(in statute miles to the nearest mile)

	The west end of the Cape May Canal	The mouth of the Mullica River	Ship John Shoal Lighthouse	Delaware River at the C&D Canal & Salem
	16			
	29	20		
	55	39	19	

channel at low tide, but once inside, the Salem River runs deep. As one travels up the Salem River, the Penn State Marina is on the left. One can also take the cut at the Salem River entrance, and just after the cut, the Salem Boat Basin is to the right.

On the Delaware River in the Salem area, the traveler has the choice of heading west to the Chesapeake Bay by way of the C&D or north up the Delaware River to Philadelphia and eventually the head of navigation at Trenton.

In the final chapter, we'll continue our cruise up the western water boundary of New Jersey—the Delaware River—to Philadelphia and beyond.

Chapter Nine

The Delaware River to Trenton

*T*he Delaware River is bounded near its mouth by the states of New Jersey and Delaware, and farther north it runs between Pennsylvania and New Jersey, up to the tri-state rock that's located in the river near Port Jervis, New York. North of Port Jervis, at Hancock, New York, the river separates into the east and west branches, and these branches originate as small, clear, sparkling streams out of the Catskill Mountains in upstate New York. From its origins in the Catskills to its confluence with Delaware Bay, the river runs free for 330 miles, but the head of navigation is near Trenton, at the so-called falls (a series of rapids) and our cruise will take us up the river to that point.

The Delaware River is like three different rivers: the clear, unspoiled northern headwaters, where it's a shallow river of rapids and white water flowing through woods and farmland; the busy industrial central section, where it's a major petroleum center for the East Coast; and the wide estuary at the south, where the river combines with and loses its identity in Delaware Bay.

The lower Delaware River is a major commercial waterway. Its origin as a route for merchandising and barter began in the early seventeenth century, when the Dutch East India Company began establishing trading posts along its banks. The earliest Dutch maps of the Delaware River employ the same *Suydt,* or south, to differentiate it from the North River, or the Hudson.

Across the river from Salem, New Jersey, at the southern end of the Delaware River, is the entrance to the Chesapeake and Delaware Canal, the 12-mile-long canal that joins the Delaware River with the north end of Chesapeake Bay (chart 9.1). The C&D, first proposed in 1661 by Dutch cartographer Augustine Herman, became a pet project of Benjamin Franklin's after the Revolution. Construction of a narrow waterway was begun, and the canal was finally opened in 1829.

The canal has changed considerably since those early days of mule power and locks, and today is a wide, lock-free, easily navigated waterway, 450-feet wide, that can handle major shipping. Red flashing traffic lights at each end of

The Delaware River entrance to the C&D Canal

the canal indicate when the canal is closed, and the dispatcher at Chesapeake City reports conditions every thirty minutes on Ch-13. When transiting the canal, sailboats must use auxiliary power, and anchoring in the canal is prohibited.

On the west shore of the Delaware River, 2 miles northwest of the C&D, one will find Delaware City, Delaware, which is a convenient place for reprovisioning. It is reached by taking Bulkhead Shoal Channel, to the south of Pea Patch Island, and then by entering the Delaware City Branch Canal. At low tide the town dock near the entrance is suitable only for dinghies, but a little further on, just before the fixed bridge, is the Delaware City Marina. It usually has space for transients, and from here it is a couple of blocks into town, where there are small grocery stores, a drugstore, a deli, a restaurant, a pizzeria, a liquor store, and antique shops.

In the town, near the river, there is also a ferry dock that provides passenger service to the Fort Delaware State Park on Pea Patch Island and to Finns Point, on the New Jersey shore. The ferry operates on weekends and holidays from the end of June to the end of September, and it also operates on Wednesday, Thursday, and Friday, from the middle of June to the beginning of September.

At the fort on Pea Patch Island, authentically clad guides take visitors back in time to the days of the Civil War and recount stories about the fort's role in

Chart 9.1 The C&D Canal, Salem River, and Pea Patch Island (reproduced from NOAA's Chart #12311)

Fort Delaware on Pea Patch Island

history. There is a museum on the island, and observation platforms overlook the largest nesting site for wading birds on the East Coast.

As we cruise north on the Delaware from the junction of the C&D, New Castle Range takes us close to the eastern side of Pea Patch Island, home of the infamous Civil War prison, Fort Delaware, that has been called the Andersonville of the north. It is now part of the Delaware State Park system.

Construction of the granite fort on Pea Patch Island began in 1846. Six thousand wooden pilings were used for its foundation. It was completed in 1860 and was designed to protect the Delaware River to the north from Confederate attack. The fort's history, however, was destined to be less than heroic. In spite of its intended role as a proud citadel charged with protecting the river north to Philadelphia, it was turned into a prison camp for Confederate soldiers and Union deserters. The first prisoners to arrive, from Stonewall Jackson's command, were lodged in the dungeons and soon the camp housed more than 12,000 prisoners, making it the largest prison camp in the country. The fort was ill-suited to this purpose. The prisoners were malnourished and plagued with disease, and a large percentage of both prisoners and the Union garrison died. The dead are buried at the Fort Mott Civil War burial ground at Finns Point, located on the New Jersey shore directly east of Pea Patch Island. A monument at Finns Point is a miniature reproduction of the Washington

The Confederate Soldiers' monument at Finns point

The Union garrison's monument at Finns Point

Monument and commemorates the 2,436, mostly unknown, Confederate soldiers who died while imprisoned on Pea Patch Island. Each year on April 26, the Daughters of the Confederacy hold a wreath-laying ceremony at the site. There is also a smaller monument to the 135 members of the Union garrison who died.

There is a dock at Finns Point that is used for the Pea Patch Island ferry boat, but it cannot be used by recreational craft. Nevertheless, there is reasonably deep water off the channel for anchoring close to shore. Double-check the chart first so that you don't anchor in the underwater cable area between the mainland and Pea Patch Island or in the path of the ferry. A dinghy can be taken to the sandy shore-beach, but keep an eye out for the nearly buried remains of granite groins that were put in to stabilize the shoreline.

The fortifications of Fort Mott, which was named for New Jersey native General Gershom Mott, are just across the open field from the river bank. The Civil War burial ground and monuments are nearly a mile away. Ask the park ranger for directions.

Although the three-fort defense system for this part of the Delaware River was designed in 1794, the bulwarks now standing at Fort Mott date from 1896 and were built as Spanish-American War fortifications, but were never used for that purpose. The other two forts that dominated the river were Fort Delaware, on Pea Patch Island, and a fort on the waterfront at Delaware City, Delaware.

During World War I, Pea Patch Island was pulled into another war effort. It was feared that the Port of Philadelphia and the ship-building yards and oil refineries south of the city might come under enemy attack so, during the summer of 1917, a net made of steel chains was designed as a U-boat deterrent. It stretched across the river from Pea Patch Island to Finns Point. It couldn't, however, stand up to a fierce early winter storm and ice-flows that year, and it was swept away.

As we continue our trip up the Delaware River, we pass between historic Pea Patch Island, Delaware, and Finns Point, New Jersey. At Finns Point the river makes an almost 90 degree bend toward the northeast, after which the state of Delaware is on both sides of the river. "Impossible," you might say; "New Jersey is on the east bank." It is true nonetheless. Although not shown on the nautical chart, an aberration in the original definition of the border between the states of New Jersey and Delaware causes the boundary line to cut through the Killcohook National Wildlife Preserve on the western tip of Finns point, so that a large section of that shoreline belongs to the state of Delaware. This same anomaly causes the northern tip of Artificial Island, north of the nuclear plants, to be part of Delaware. If you don't believe it, check a good road map or atlas for confirmation.

Finns Point is the home of one of New Jersey's least known yet most historic lighthouses, built to mark the sharp turn in the river and used as an artillery observation post. It was constructed in 1876, and it is hard to see from the river. After its restoration in the 1980s, it was added to the National Register of Historic Places.

On the lower Delaware River and the upper Delaware Bay the various channels are termed ranges, and the buoys in these channels display a letter that denotes the range. Thus, buoys on the New Castle Range carry the suffix N, on the Deepwater point Range a D, and on the Cherry Island Range a C, and so on.

Delaware River tidal currents can have a significant effect on the speed-over-the-bottom of auxiliaries or other boats of displacement-hull design, and can cut the true speed almost in half. Further up the river, ebb tides are of an even greater velocity, since tidal currents and river flow are added together. As an example, the tides at New Castle, which are three and a half to four hours after those at the entrance to Delaware Bay, cause a 1.9 knot flood tide (going up river) and a 2.4 knot ebb tide (flowing down river.)

As we approach the industrialized section of the Delaware River, debris in the water increases, especially after heavy rainstorms. For those in search of a bucolic setting, this is not the place, but it is interesting. When looking up river, we can see the high twin bridges of the Delaware Memorial Bridge at the southern end of the New Jersey Turnpike. Since there are few small-craft facilities along this stretch of the Delaware, it is good to know that up the Christina River in Wilmington, and completely out of sight, are recreational marinas. The Delaware-Pennsylvania border reaches the river just south of the Sun Oil refinery at Marcus Hook. At this point the boundary line between the states returns to midriver. Across from Marcus Hook an anchorage exists on the New Jersey side of the channel; it is for tankers awaiting their turn at the docks on the west side of the river. It is a good idea to monitor Ch-16 and Ch-13 and to keep a wary eye on ship movements when transiting this area.

The next bridge crosses the Delaware between Chester, Pennsylvania, and Bridgeport, New Jersey. About 4 miles beyond this bridge there are small craft facilities on the Pennsylvania shore behind the 2-mile-long Little Tinicum Island, in the town of Essington, Pennsylvania. These marinas are just off the ends of the runways of the Philadelphia International Airport. Although it is a convenient place for refueling, it is not the quietest place to spend the night, since flights are landing and taking off overhead every minute.

Infrequently, small waterspouts have occurred in this area, apparently resulting from a vortex created by the jet traffic. They have occasionally done damage to boat covers and bimini tops. On the positive side, the several

Heavy shipping vessels join us as we head up the Delaware River

The Delaware Memorial Bridge across the Delaware River emerges from fog

The Pennsylvania shore near Marcus Hook

marinas there have fuel, supplies, and haul-out, and can handle hull and engine repairs. In addition, Little Tinicum Island provides protection from the river wakes.

Just north of the Philadelphia airport the Schuylkill River flows into the Delaware. The river was named by the Dutch, and translates to hidden creek. The Schuylkill runs through the center of Philadelphia, and the area around its mouth, at the confluence of the Delaware, has become the center of the petroleum and ship-building industry at the Port of Philadelphia. Just north of the Schuylkill, on the Pennsylvania shore, was the site of the impressive Philadelphia Navy Yard, which maintained naval ships of all descriptions at dockside or in dry dock and was in service for many decades. The Navy Yard was decommissioned in the late 1990s.

In 1681 William Penn, son of an admiral, was given a grant from the crown for lands west of the Delaware River. The northern section of these lands was named Pennsylvania, and after the Revolution, a hundred years later, the southern section was named Delaware. When William Penn first arrived at this primitive land in his ship *Welcome,* he landed north of where the Schuylkill joins the Delaware, where the water was deep right up to shore. Penns Landing, as it was later named, is located at that site in what is now Philadelphia.

There, in the proverbial middle of nowhere, Penn discovered that the Blue Anchor Tavern was already doing a thriving business.

Naturally, in the 1700s there were no bridges across this wide section of the Delaware, below Trenton. This didn't deter the American Indians, who had been navigating and crossing the river for thousands of years on log rafts, canoes, and inflated animal intestines.

With the arrival of the Europeans, large ships traveled the river, which was now used as a highway of business, commerce, and colonization. The principle commercial product of the area in colonial times was flour, and the streams flowing into the Delaware, such as the Schuylkill, provided the water power to grind it. In those early years, water-borne cargo was threatened by attack; privateers, American Indians, and pirates marauded Delaware Bay from Cape Henlopen to the lower Delaware River. One of the pirates was Edward Teach, or Blackbeard, who was so bold as to buy his supplies in Philadelphia, well aware that the Quaker pacifists would do him no harm.

By the 1940s and 1950s, and before the promulgation of stringent federal and state pollution regulations, the Delaware River in the Philadelphia and Camden vicinity was in poor shape from an ecological standpoint. Water quality had already begun declining as far back as the 1700s, only about one hundred years after Henry Hudson discovered the Delaware. Then, the biggest polluters on the waterway were ships and the activity on wharves, but in the later 1800s ship building, manufacturing, oil refineries, and a massive population growth sent the water into a rapid decline. The problem was compounded during World War II, when the importance of shipbuilding and oil production superseded that of the environment. All of the waste from the new industries, as well as sewage from the exploding population, were dumped into the river and its tributaries. The water quality was so bad that ships at dockside had paint stripped from their hulls by the corrosive mixture.

Something clearly had to be done, and it started with a New Jersey, New York, Pennsylvania, and Delaware advisory commission, the Interstate Commission on the Delaware River Basin. The newly implemented environmental laws enabled the commission to set up water standards and cleanup programs.

Now the river quality is improving noticeably each year, and environmental advocacy groups such as the Watershed Association of the Delaware River and the Delaware Riverkeeper plan to continue the fight. The Delaware River is one of the many bodies of water nationwide that has a keeper. The Delaware Riverkeeper organization, affiliated with the American Littoral Society, has been working since 1988 to change the face of stewardship of the river through monitoring by volunteers from Hancock, New York, to Delaware Bay.

Although the river, in its industrial lower reaches, might seem devoid of aquatic life, shad use these waters as a pathway to the upper reaches of the Delaware all the way to New York State, where they spawn in the spring. Then the young shad, during their fall migration, swim down, past the oil refineries, and past the wild marshes of Delaware Bay, back to the ocean.

As we round the next bend on the river, we see the Walt Whitman Bridge, which joins Philadelphia to Gloucester City, New Jersey. Farther up-river, beyond the Walt Whitman Bridge, the Ben Franklin Bridge joins Philadelphia and Camden.

In 1898 vacationers from both Philadelphia and Camden began using the newly completed 55-mile-long railroad link from Camden to Atlantic City. The trains regularly made the trip in fifty minutes, racing through the New Jersey Pine Barrens, with smoke billowing from their stacks at speeds of more than 60 miles an hour. (The round-trip fare at the time was one dollar.) A 1920 railroad report revealed that of the sixteen fastest trains in the world, thirteen were on the Camden–Atlantic City run.

On the Philadelphia waterfront, Penns Landing rivals New York's South Street Seaport. In the boat basin one will find an outstanding collection of historic ships: a World War II submarine, the USS *Becuna,* which participated in World War II in the South Pacific, as well as in the Korean and Vietnam wars;

Penns Landing at Philadelphia

a tug boat; and Commodore Dewey's flagship from the 1898 battle of Manila Bay, the USS *Olympia,* which carried twenty-six cannons and eight torpedo tubes. When standing on the bridge of the Olympia you'll see footprints painted on the deck. It was at this spot that Commodore Dewey gave the famous command, "You may fire when you are ready, Gridley," which led to the defeat of the Spanish in Manila Bay. At Penns Landing there is also the tall sailing ship *Gazela,* a 177-foot-long square-rigged sailing ship built in 1883. The *Gazela* was the oldest tall ship to participate in the 1976 Tall Ship Festival in New York Harbor. You will also find *The Spirit of Philadelphia,* as well as other small boats.

Just north of these historic ships is the Independence Seaport Museum, which opened in 1995. The museum celebrates the ancient arts of the mariner with wonderful displays that should not be missed by any boater. The museum also offers workshops that teach the art of crafting small wooden boats, as well as other nautical crafts. Close to the museum is a multitiered, tree-lined amphitheater, where concerts and festivals are held, as well as a sculpture garden.

Penns Landing has an eighty-slip marina for recreational boats of up to 40 feet long, where dock space for transients is sometimes available (chart 9.2).

Commodore Dewey's flagship *Olympia* at Penns Landing (photo courtesy of Rusty Kennedy, Independence Seaport Museum, Philadelphia, Pa.)

In the last few years Philadelphia has become a leading cruise-ship port, and frequently these ships will be docked at the Penns Landing pier, adding to the intriguing maritime atmosphere.

In the Philadelphia-Camden area the RiverLink Ferry System, a shuttle-ferry, is a convenient way of traveling back and forth across the river and provides a quick and pleasant passage between Penns Landing and the New Jersey State Aquarium in Camden. The ferry runs seven days a week, every forty minutes during the day in the summertime, and the 2,500-foot trip across the river takes less than ten minutes. For further information on the ferry's operating hours call: 215-925-LINK or check: riverlinkferry.org.

The RiverLink also connects Penns Landing, Camden Children's Garden, Tweeter Center (in Camden), the Camden baseball field, and the USS *New Jersey*, as well as the New Jersey State Aquarium.

For those who would like to visit the USS *New Jersey*, it is docked on the river near the Camden aquarium—within walking distance. A shuttle-bus to the battleship is also available in front of the aquarium.

The Battleship USS *New Jersey* had her keel laid in the Philadelphia Navy Yard in 1940 and was launched December 7, 1942, a year to the day after the attack on Pearl Harbor. She was christened by Mrs. Charles Edison, daughter-

The USS *New Jersey*, on the Delaware River at Camden (photo courtesy of Jesse N. Lebovics)

in-law of the famous New Jersey inventor, Thomas Edison. After her commissioning in the spring of 1943, the USS *New Jersey* headed to the Pacific, where her exploits led to her becoming our nation's most decorated battleship. She also took part in the Korean and Vietnam wars until her decommissioning in February 1991. After her decommissioning, the battleship completed her final voyage from Bremerton, Washington, to the former Philadelphia Ship Yard, arriving on Veteran's Day 1999. The ship, now berthed in Camden, is a floating museum, where history comes to life as visitors experience a two-hour guided tour through the Iowa-class ship—one of the largest battleships ever built.

The Home Port Alliance, the organization responsible for bringing the battleship *New Jersey* home, also provides educational programs, navy reunions, special events, and volunteering opportunities.

Across the river in Philadelphia there are several marinas available to the recreational boater. These are located just south and north of the Ben Franklin Bridge. To the south of the bridge and north of Penns Landing, the jointly owned Pier-3 Marina and Pier-5 Marina usually monitor Ch-16. Both marinas have slips for transients with laundry, showers, and rest rooms, with a deli and a restaurant nearby. Slips have water, electricity, and cable-TV. The marina is secured with locked entrance gates and digital access codes. Transient boaters should make advance reservations and a deposit for the first night may be required along with the reservation.

From these marinas it is a short walk into what is sometimes called America's most historic square mile. A good place to begin is the Visitor's Center on Chestnut and 3rd streets, close to Independence Hall, the Liberty Bell, and the Betsy Ross house. Long lines can be expected at Philadelphia's important historical sites during the height of the tourist season. Shopping, restaurants, hotels, and banks, can also be found nearby.

The Pier-3 and Pier-5 marinas are located between existing piers that were formerly used for commercial shipping. These piers have been converted into condominiums, overlooking the marinas. Entrance into the marinas is by way of two right-angle turns, designed to reduce wakes from river traffic.

Just to the north of the Ben Franklin Bridge the Philadelphia Marine Center offers a 300-slip marina for boats up to 150 feet in length. It has a complete range of amenities including car rentals, cable-TV, telephone hookups at dockside, showers, and a Laundromat. Marina security is established with a locked gate at the land entrance.

Across the river from Philadelphia, the Thomas H. Kean State Aquarium at Camden is another one of the biggest attractions on the Camden waterfront. The facility was funded by the New Jersey State Legislature and was opened in 1992. It rivals the aquarium at Baltimore's Inner Harbor. The huge main tank

Chart 9.2 The Philadelphia-Camden area (reproduced from NOAA's Chart #12312)

within the building contains over three-quarters of a million gallons of "sea water," which is made from tap water, salt and trace elements. It is the largest aquarium tank in the United States, with the exception of the one located at the EPCOT Center in Florida.

The first floor of the aquarium focuses on aquatic life from New Jersey waters, and the second floor features marine life from around the world. Other displays include cascading waterfalls, ocean surf, touch-tanks, and a trout stream. There is a one and a half acre park surrounding the aquarium, with an outside seal pool, and the Riverside Cafe is on the deck of the aquarium, overlooking the Delaware and the Philadelphia skyline.

Adjoining the Camden Aquarium to the south is the Wiggins Park Camden County Marina. The marina has floating docks, around-the-clock security, water, electricity, a picnic area, and it monitors Ch-16 and Ch-68. This facility has transient, seasonal, monthly, daily, and even hourly rates (for those who would like to stop off by boat and visit the aquarium or the USS *New Jersey*). If planning to stay overnight, one should arrive at the marina before closing time, since the gate surrounding the marina is then locked and only boaters with keys have access. The marina is in the form of a complete circle, with slips around its periphery and rolling lawns separating it from the aquarium.

The RiverLink from Penns Landing, approaching the Camden Aquarium

The Camden Aquarium (photo, top, courtesy of Linda Riley, the New Jersey State Aquarium at Camden)

At the top of the hill between the two, a brick common surrounded by tables is used for picnics and provides a wonderful panorama of all the places we have mentioned.

Walt Whitman spent much of his time on the Delaware River and found the scene comprising the Camden-Philadelphia ferry operators, the river's waterfowl, and the "full-starr'd, blue-black night" one that "speak(s) no word, nothing to the intellect, yet so eloquent, so communicative to the soul."

Walt Whitman (1819–1892) spent the last eight years of his life in his home at 330 Mickle Boulevard in Camden. The house, purchased with the royalties from *Leaves of Grass,* was close enough to the river that Whitman could watch the tall ships cruising by. His home was one of Camden's most important museums until it burned to the ground in September 1994.

Back on board, after an interesting day or two ashore, we will now head north from the Philadelphia-Camden area. Here, the Delaware becomes slightly less industrialized on both shores. The main channel heads west of Petty Island, and just beyond is a ConRail railroad bridge with a lift span that has a charted down-clearance of 49 feet. The Betsy Ross Highway bridge is just beyond. Skippers of sailboats would be wise to call ahead to the ConRail bridge tender on Ch-13 to request the actual bridge clearance.

Two miles further upriver, owners of large sailboats should also note the 53-foot closed clearance of the bridge at Palmyra. In these upper parts of the Delaware River's navigable waters it is important to remember that freshets can raise the river levels considerably higher than normal. Bridge boards on the abutments to bridges should be checked for real clearance before you commit to a passage. During March and April, due to melting snow and ice breakup, freshets can cause the river to rise as much as 10 to 20 feet above mean low water at Trenton, and even heavy summertime rainstorms can cause a 9-foot rise. The maximum recorded freshet rises have been 21.5 feet at Trenton, 19.5 feet at Bordentown, and 13 feet at Bristol.

In these reaches of the river the tides, especially at times of high water or when the tide is ebbing, are fast flowing and an auxiliary or displacement hull will have a hard time making progress against them. For those operating auxiliaries or displacement hulls, it would be wise to plan the trip in conjunction with a tide table.

Just above the Palmyra Bridge, on the New Jersey shore, we come to the town of Riverton. In 1865 the founding fathers of Riverton agreed that they would organize the first yacht club on the Delaware. They employed the Riverton Iron Pier for the purpose, which was also used by the side-wheel vessel that ferried passengers to and from Philadelphia. The club, dedicated in July of 1865, is still very much active with sailboat races, instruction for children, and regattas. Many national and world sailing champions have graduated from the yacht club's enthusiastic sailing program.

Dredge Harbor, on the New Jersey side of the river and about 8 miles above the Ben Franklin Bridge, offers five marinas and a large selection of small-craft services and facilities. If at all possible, it would be a good idea to make advance reservations for dock space at these marinas, since they seldom monitor the VHF band.

Dredge Harbor is also the home of the Cherubini Boat Company, which manufactures fiberglass sailboats and has the distinction of being the only fiberglass schooner manufacturer in the world. The schooner rig, which is seldom seen today, was once the rig of choice for much of America's coastal commerce until the early part of this century. I must admit to being biased toward the schooner rig, as I consider it the prettiest sailing rig ever developed.

Just upriver from Dredge Harbor, on the New Jersey side of the river and about 6 miles north of Camden, we come to Rancocas Creek. It was named for the American Indian tribe that lived on its shores. The creek originates in Lebanon State Forest and flows through the high wooded shores to Mount Holly, where it changes to a lowland tidewater stream before joining the Delaware. This is a creek with deep water, where local boaters frequently anchor. If you decide to drop the hook here, be sure to stay out of the channel, since there is sand-and-gravel barge traffic as far as the first bridge. There are small-craft facilities on the north shore of the creek, just before the first bridge, as well as up river at Bridgeboro.

About 4 miles farther up the Delaware, on the Pennsylvania side, just beyond Neshaminy Creek, there is a state marina on the Pennsylvania side of the river. Although the marina welcomes transients, space can be very limited at the height of the season. Several more boatyards are located further up Neshaminy Creek, within three-quarters of a mile from its mouth.

The quaint town of Burlington, New Jersey, about 7 miles beyond Dredge Harbor, was a bustling mercantile port presided over by Quaker business men three hundred years ago. (In 1789, James Fenimore Cooper was born in a two-story stuccoed house on Main Street, which is now owned by the Burlington County Historical Society.) Now, Burlington resembles the quintessential small town at the turn of the century. Tours are provided through historic homes, and there are established parks along most of Burlington's Delaware River waterfront.

To the north of the town the Delaware separates around Burlington Island, where the west side of the island is the main channel. Skippers of sailboats who are considering gunkholing around the east side should take note of the 45-foot power lines across the waterway.

The Cherubini Boat Company at Dredge Harbor

On the east side of Burlington Island, about a half mile up and just beyond the Assiscunk Creek, is the Curtin Marina, with docks and mooring buoys. It has a marine store, engine repairs, a canvas shop, and a restaurant overlooking the water.

Two miles north of Burlington Island the Delaware takes a 90 degree turn to the east at Florence Bend. At this point we are about 9 miles below the head of navigation at Trenton. The town of Florence is on the New Jersey shore, and across the river in Tullytown is Tullytown Cove, a basin about one thousand yards long, with a narrow entrance off the river. The entrance is about a quarter of a mile north of the large yellow fuel tank on the Pennsylvania shore. It is a locally popular anchorage, protected from the wash of river traffic. As a point of reference, there's a large park sloping down to the river in Florence, directly across the river from Tullytown Cove.

Bordentown is about 7 miles upriver from Florence Bend, on a high bank on the southeastern side of the entrance to Crosswicks Creek. It is one of central New Jersey's oldest settlements. In 1751 Joseph Borden Jr. started the first weekly sailing packet line that provided a connection between Philadelphia and the New Jersey stagecoach line to Perth Amboy. Once at Perth Amboy, the passengers boarded a sailboat for the final leg of their journey to New York City. The trip from Philadelphia to New York took three days, considered

The entrance to Tullytown Cove

breakneck speed at the time. Bordentown, the exchange point between stage-coach and sailboat, developed from this early venture. In later years it became the terminus for another mode of transportation along the Delaware and Raritan Canal (discussed in chapter 2), which was closed in 1932.

The roster of Bordentown citizens includes such notables as Clara Barton, founder of the American Red Cross; Francis Hopkinson, a signer of the Declaration of Independence; and Joseph, the eldest brother of Napoleon Bonaparte. Joseph had been King of Naples and then King of Spain. When his brother's reign came to an end, he fled to America in disguise. He purchased more than one thousand acres of land near Bordentown, on a high hill overlooking the river, and named it Port Breeze. Only the land now exists, since the original buildings were destroyed by fire. During his fourteen years in Bordentown, Joseph contributed much to the community and was well liked.

In 1790, years before Fulton's much-publicized steamboat service on the Hudson River, John Fitch established a steamboat service on the Delaware between Bordentown, New Jersey, and Philadelphia. The steamboat ran a regular schedule with few breakdowns, and the 25-mile trip could be made in four hours.

At Borentown the river takes a 90 degree turn to the west, and the head of navigation at Trenton is only a few miles up river. Up Crosswicks Creek in

Bordentown, just beyond the new highway bridge, two membership-only yacht clubs can be seen from the river.

About 3 miles north of Bordentown, Ross Marine Service can be found on the New Jersey shore about 2 miles south of Trenton. It is immediately north of the Public Service Electric and Gas complex, which is easily identified by the two tall chimneys. Ross Marine usually has slips for transients, with about 4 feet of water at low tide. From this location there is nothing within walking or easy biking distance.

Within view of the bridges at Trenton that mark the end of our voyage up the Delaware, there is a high concrete bulkhead along the New Jersey shore. It was used during World War II for loading heavy equipment aboard ships. The Trenton Marine Center is at the southern end of this bulkhead. It has a floating dock parallel to the shoreline in 25–30 feet of water, a boat elevator on the face of the bulkhead for launching and retrieving small craft, engine repair services, parts, and a marine supply store. It frequently can provide an overnight berth for transients. At the north end of this same bulkhead there is a town park, where you'll see locals using long lines to fish down the vertical 30-foot concrete face that rises from the river.

Along the final mile of the passage to the bridges at Trenton, be careful not to stray west of the marked channel; there are submerged rocks all along the Pennsylvania side of the river.

The head of navigation on the Delaware River at Trenton

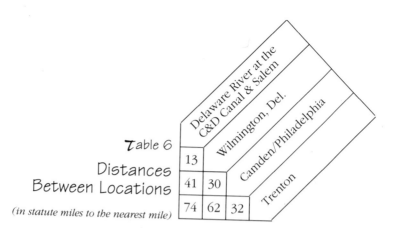

Table 6

Distances
Between Locations

(in statute miles to the nearest mile)

Delaware River at the C&D Canal & Salem	Wilmington, Del.	Camden/Philadelphia	Trenton
13			
41	30		
74	62	32	

Washington Crossing is located 7 miles north of Trenton. On Christmas night of 1776, Washington and his army, almost in rags, crossed the river in small boats to attack the Hessians. The towns on both sides of the river at this point, both in New Jersey and Pennsylvania, were named Washington Crossing. The event was immortalized by artist Emanuel Leutze in his famous painting, which has been replicated on New Jersey twenty-five-cent coins.

Downstream from Washington's Crossing, and just north of the bridge in Trenton, there is a series of rapids, the Great Falls of the Delaware. Above the rapids the river is fresh, and below the rapids it's tidal and brackish. The tidal range at Trenton is nearly 8 feet, the highest in New Jersey. Trenton is on a latitude just 12 nautical miles south of Sandy Hook, which is 42 miles away, across the narrow neck of New Jersey. To reach Sandy Hook by water is quite another matter; it's a trip of 260 miles. It is little wonder that the Delaware and Raritan Canal was so popular before it was replaced by the railroads and highways of today.

At this spot the last navigational buoy (which is just south of the Amtrak railroad bridge that joins the capital of New Jersey with Pennsylvania) marks the head of navigation on the Delaware River. This buoy also marks the end of our cruise of New Jersey's navigable waterways. Although we have covered the major tidewater arteries, there are still hundreds of other side trips left to make—opportunities to explore and gunkhole on New Jersey waters are boundless. Will I see you on the water?

General Information for Cruising

*T*he Responsibilities of the Skipper

It is the responsibility and duty of the skipper on a small boat to learn the job of being a skipper. Study, thought, and prudence are prerequisites, and until the skipper has gained enough experience, conservatism is the key. As the saying goes, "It's better to be an old sailor than a bold sailor."

The fate of those on the water depends on the type and condition of the vessel as well as on the crew. Just as with a chain, the weakest link determines its strength, regardless of the condition of the rest of the chain. So whenever preparing for a cruise in a small boat, there are certain prerequisites in both hardware and mental software. Some suggestions are:

1. Have up-to-date charts on board. Learn how to read them, and use them.

2. If the cruising plans include an offshore passage, alert someone on shore regarding the itinerary of the planned trip, along with expected times of arrival and proposed check-ins.

3. Brief the crew and passengers on safety gear before shoving off. Show them where the life jackets and fire extinguishers are located and how to use them. Explain how to use the throwable flotation devices. Also determine if there are any nonswimmers aboard. Establish rules for wearing life jackets for both nonswimmers and children.

4. Briefly explain man-overboard procedures. If everyone aboard, apart from the skipper are relatively inexperienced, show the most knowledgeable how to stop the boat when under power or sail. Also explain, as simply as possible, how to make an emergency call on the VHF radio.

5. If aboard a sailboat, describe the special things to watch out for, including the results of an accidental jibe.

6. Check the weather conditions before leaving and again when out on the water.

7. Have prescribed safety equipment on board, including the correct number and size of life jackets for all passengers and crew members.

8. Have adequate anchors and anchor line.

9. Make sure the navigation lights are operational.

10. Be sure the fuel supply is adequate for the proposed trip.

11. If trailering to a launching ramp, check out the trailer, lights, safety chains, and bearings.

12. Know the height above water of the tallest part of the boat, so there is no indecision when approaching bridges. At all bridges, there are bridge-height boards fastened to the abutments bordering the navigable opening. The numbers at the water's surface indicate the actual clearance from water to bridge. Due to tides, wind, or rainfall, this is often different from the charted clearance.

13. Finally, abide by the rules of the road, and don't forget common courtesy.

Until a few years ago, getting help when your boat was disabled was as simple as calling the Coast Guard, but in the 1980s the policy of the Coast Guard was changed, with a mandate that nonemergency calls would not be handled by Coast Guard personnel. These nonemergency situations including running out of fuel, having engine problems, or running aground when there is no injury to the people on board and the situations are not life threatening. The void in obtaining help in these situations has been filled by commercial towing companies, which now handle all nonemergency situations. Boaters asking for assistance (make a general call for a tow on Ch-16) should expect to pay more than $100 an hour from the time the towboat leaves its dock until it returns. This can make a weekend error in judgment rather expensive, since the average tow usually involves at least a two to three hour operation. To ease these unexpected contingencies, yearly towing insurance policies can be obtained, and some boating organizations include towing insurance as part of their membership fee.

Also, be aware that if a friendly boater offers to give you a tow for a fee— it is illegal. Before anyone can accept money for towing, the person towing is required to obtain a Coast Guard Towing License.

Safety on board is important in other ways, which are more personal but are serious nonetheless. When out on the water, sunburn is an all too common occurrence. Reflection from the water and the deck subjects the body to more sun intensity than one would be subjected to if on the beach. It is a good idea to keep a high-number sunscreen on board—one with both UVA and UVB inhibitors. We also keep a supply of wide-brimmed hats with tethers on board for those guests who have forgotten to bring their own.

It is always a good idea for the boat skipper to find out if anyone has a history of motion sickness. We keep Bonine and Dramamine on board, as well as acupressure wristbands, and electronic wristbands, which many prefer and find effective. For extended periods on the water—many hours or several days at sea—the behind-the-ear Transderm Scop patch is very effective, but this requires a doctor's prescription.

Since all medications produce possible negative side effects, it is important that the directions be read and understood. As an example, most people find that taking a small amount of alcohol, even many hours after a

Bonine tablet, makes it almost impossible to stay awake. In the case of pregnant women, children, those with medical problems, and those on other medications, understanding the limitations of seasick remedies is especially important.

Before modern day medications, ginger was the remedy for nausea. In fact, ginger ale was developed as a cure for an upset stomach and is well worth a try.

For most who are prone to mal-de-mer, keeping their eyes on the horizon and avoiding reading or going below is all that is necessary. Many others develop immunity after prolonged time on the water, while still others (including Britain's foremost seaman in the late eighteenth century, Admiral Horatio Nelson), get seasick whenever on board a boat.

Most important of all, it is the responsibility of the skipper to do his or her homework. When on a cruise or boat delivery, my nightly routine consists of going over the proposed route for the next day. Some of the things I check for are channel depths, bridge heights and opening times, potential storm anchorages, sources of fuel and supplies, and interesting and safe stopover spots for the next night. I mark my charts with the appropriate notes, which is not only a great help the following day but a source of information for future cruises. We always keep a selection of navigational information on board, and I have included a list of suggested publications later in this chapter.

It is common for skippers who are about to start a voyage to a new area or on a new body of water to feel apprehensive. This is especially true for the novice who is about to begin an ocean passage for the first time. A little fear and anxiety is good. It keeps the adrenaline pumping and prompts preplanning and alertness. Too much fear, however, can erode the skipper's abilities and ruin what would otherwise be an exciting voyage. Too little fear is also a bad sign; it fosters complacency. Desiderius Erasmus (1455?–1536), Dutch scholar and theologian, hit the nail on the head when he wrote: "Only the dolt showeth no fear."

Weather and Seasonal Changes on New Jersey Waters

Winter months produce the roughest seas along the New Jersey coast, with gales up to 5 percent of the time between November and March. In January, ocean waves of more than 8 feet occur up to 25 percent of the time, and 40-foot waves have been recorded.

During many of New Jersey's winters, the Intracoastal Waterway, as well as the Delaware River, can freeze solid all the way across. The ice can drag buoys off-station and can destroy or incapacitate any of New Jersey's aids to navigation. By the end of many winters 10 percent or more of the navigational aids are missing, damaged, off-station, extinguished, destroyed, or leaning, so that an early spring cruise becomes more chancy than one later in the season. In addition, winter storms may rearrange the bottom and create shoal spots across the waterway that didn't exist before, usually near inlets: These spots may not have been dredged as yet, or buoys relocated.

With the arrival of spring, wind and waves become more subdued, as the semipermanent Bermuda high begins to dominate our weather. The possibility of advection fog increases significantly in the spring as warm moist air flows across the still-cold water. May is statistically the worst month for fog, but we have frequently had our plans interrupted through late June.

Typical summer weather will include a couple of weeks of warm, humid days, with winds out of the south or southwest. During the daytime, along the intracoastal waters, a sea breeze develops about midday, and the winds shift in from the ocean. This sea breeze can add to the prevailing winds and cause higher than forecasted winds on the inland waters and along the immediate coast. On hot, humid days there is always the possibility of scattered thunderstorms, and from midsummer until October, there is a potential threat of tropical storms and hurricanes.

Fall weather typically consists of periods of dry sunny days and cool nights, and the threat of tropical storms begins to decrease. Radiation fog becomes more frequent, forming inland at night, then drifting toward the coastal waters in the early morning. This type of fog is more local than the advection fogs of spring, and it usually burns off by midday. The prevailing winds during September and October are from the northeast, a bonus for those sailboats heading south for the winter. From November to March, prevailing winds are from the northwest.

Our schooner, *Delphinus*, anchored in a dense fog for thirty-six hours in Horseshoe Cove, inside Sandy Hook

Tides and Storms

Poets and ancient cultures have long compared life itself with the tides. Along the North Sea coast of England it was believed that most deaths occurred at ebb tide, as in, "life ebbs away with the tide." Historically, a flood tide has been considered an omen of good fortune, and an ebb tide has been considered with foreboding.

Tides are created chiefly from the gravitational effects of the moon and the sun, as well as from atmospheric pressure. The wind is also an important factor and is of great importance in our area. (I will say more about the wind later.) The moon is the major force in creating tides; its gravitational pull is about two and a quarter times that of the sun, so that our tides usually "follow the moon," but are slightly modified by the gravitation of the sun. The gravitational effects of the moon and the sun generally create two high and two low tides every day in the northeast.

The moon rotates around the earth so that it passes over the same longitude about once every twenty-four hours and fifty minutes. This means that at any given location, tides occur about fifty minutes later every day. If you see high tide at a particular location at 9 a.m. Monday morning, you can expect a high tide to occur there at 9:50 a.m. Tuesday morning, at 10:40 a.m. Wednesday morning, and so on.

When the sun and the moon are in line with the earth, which happens at the time of a new moon or a full moon, the gravitational pull is greater than average, and so called spring tides occur. In this case, spring does not refer to the time of year but rather the welling-up of the water, as from a spring. When the sun and the moon are at right angles to the earth, with the moon in its first or third quarter, the gravitational pulls tend to cancel out slightly, and we have less than average, or neap tides.

The tides created by the gravitation of the sun and moon are called celestial tides, as opposed to those tidal effects created by atmospheric pressure or the wind. Printed tide tables, as well as tide computer programs, allow the celestial tides to be calculated years in advance. One of the things these tables and programs can't show us, however, is the effect of atmospheric pressure and wind on the tides—and the wind effects are of great importance to the residents and mariners of the New Jersey shoreline.

Those cruising New Jersey's inland tidal waters, protected by the barrier islands, know that the tides there are considerably less than those on the ocean side of the barrier islands. This is due to the narrow inlets that limit the exchanged of water between the ocean and the intracoastal waters. This limited water exchange causes low tides on the bays that are higher than those in the ocean, and the bay high tides to be lower than the ocean high tides. At high tide, the ocean tries to fill up the bay, but before it gets a chance, the tide has changed and begun to drop, so that the tide variations in the bay never approach those on the ocean side of the island. This also causes the times of high and low tides in the bays to lag behind those for the ocean.

Many boaters along our Atlantic coastline think it would be great if the inlets to the ocean were broad and deep—in actuality this would be a disaster.

If there were no longer a restriction of water flow between the ocean and the bay, high and low tides in the bay would be the same as those in the ocean. At low tide a large percentage of the bottom of the Intracoastal Waterway would be exposed, and most of the recreational activities on the water, not to mention much of the bay's ecology, would cease to exist. High tides in the bays, with water levels the same as in the ocean, would create flooding comparable to that of a nor'easter or a hurricane. Under these conditions people would not be able to live on most of the barrier islands or on the mainland side of the bays. So when people complain about our inlets, I say. "I'll take them just as they are, thank you very much."

But why do the nor'easters seem to cause trouble for those barrier islands and inland bays, even more than hurricanes; and why don't the narrow inlets protect the bays?

During an extended blow, such as the nor'easters of 1962, 1991, 1992, and 1993, a different scenario takes place. During a long blow (twelve hours or more) an ocean current is produced by the wind. The rule of thumb is that this current is about 2 percent of the wind speed, so that during an extended blow of 60 mph toward our shore, a current of 1.2 mph is set up. This current is directed to the whole coastline and causes the water to mound up against the shore, creating higher than predicted tides. This mounding effect is very real, with the ocean water level close to the shore much higher than it is many miles out to sea. On top of this mound of water are the unusually high wind-created waves. The height of these waves is directly related to the wind speed, its duration, and the distance that these winds are blowing across the water, or the fetch. During the disastrous 1962 storm, the fetch was more than 1,000 miles.

During a nor'easter, the storm surge created by the winds and the current forces the ocean waters into the inlets; even during celestial low tide, the height of the ocean water, along with the wind, does not allow water to escape from the bays. The next ocean high tide again adds water to the bays until, after a series of high tides, the water level in the bays approaches that of high tide in the ocean.

The American Red Cross estimates that more than 10,000 homes in New Jersey were either destroyed or damaged during the December 1992 nor'easter. Many old-timers say it was the worst storm they've seen since the 1938 hurricane, and that didn't last as long. We are fortunate that most of the hurricanes that have visited this area have been rapid travelers. In a hurricane, tides are also created by the wind. In addition, the low pressure in the eye can suck up the ocean into unusually high tides, much as soda is sucked up by a straw. Fortunately, hurricanes at this latitude pass rapidly, so that the piling up of water against our coast is reduced—and remember, it usually takes more than one high tide to fill up the bays. As the eye passes by us, there is a wind shift, and water is usually blown out of the bays. The tidal effect of the wind on the inland tidewaters is commonly called blow-in and blow-out tides. Except in areas close to the inlets, they are the major cause of the varying tide heights in our intracoastal waters, and their effects are even greater than those of the moon and the sun.

National Weather Service officials characterize the December 1992 nor'easter as a one-hundred-year storm. Others dubbed it the storm of the century. Three months later the appellation was repeated and applied to the March 13, 1993 storm, along with the added distinction of the "white hurricane." This was an appropriate name, since in many ways the March storm resembled a hurricane more than it did a typical nor'easter. Satellite photographs even revealed an eye.

Let's hope that the latest one-hundred-year storm holds on to its title and receives no further challenges in the near future.

You will hear several terms used when monitoring weather information on the radio:

Mean High Water—is the average level of all the high tides measured in the last nineteen years.

Mean Low Water—is the average level of all the low tides measured in the last nineteen years.

Mean Low Low Water—needs some explanation. There are usually two low and two high tides each day. Usually one of the low tides is lower than the other that day and one of the high tides is higher than the other one that day. If we take the average of the lower of the two low tides each day, over a nineteen-year period, we have "Mean Low Low Water."

Storm Preparation

June of each year marks the official beginning of the hurricane season, however most of the hurricanes that are spawned in the tropics never find their way to our shores. Intellectually, we know that violent storms are a very real possibility, but we usually rationalize with: "It won't happen this year," and we put them in the back of our minds. But the Big Blow is not necessarily a hurricane. "The Perfect Storm"—the Halloween nor'easter of 1991—caught the forecasters by surprise, and devastated homes and boats throughout the northeast. Strong cold fronts and associated violent thunderstorms can also have devastating winds—frequently of hurricane strength. No matter where you do your boating, storms are a fact of life. But if you heard a radio announcement that a major storm would hit your area within twenty-four hours, would you have a plan of action for taking care of your boat? If you are like the vast majority of boat owners, you wouldn't. The time to plan for the onslaught is not when you hear that announcement, the time is now. Obviously our property on land is vulnerable to the winds and storm surge, but even more vulnerable, is our floating property.

Boat owners are able to go a long way toward protecting their boats, and many of these precautions can be taken when the weather is clear and calm. Begin by checking to see if your deck cleats are adequately through-bolted with substantial backup plates. Are the cleats large enough to take large-diameter storm lines, with more than one line on the same cleat? Probably not—and they need to be changed. Will the chocks also handle these storm lines when they are encased in chafing gear? Do you have large size mooring lines made up to the proper length, with eye-splices that will fit your cleats? All these chores take time, and when a storm is approaching, that's one thing that's in short supply.

On all boats, but especially on sailboats, one of the most important things that can be done is to reduce windage by removing all the sails, especially roller-furling headsails, and certainly the dodger, as well as any other canvas on board. Even seemingly innocuous halyards create wind resistance. A half-inch halyard going to the top of a 50-foot mast presents 4 square feet of resistance to the wind—an enormous pressure in hurricane winds. Booms on sailboats that can be easily removed can be stowed in the cabin. On very small sailboats unstepping the mast is a good idea. Anything on deck that can't be removed should be lashed down firmly. Vulnerable antennas should be taken off and plastic compass and instrument gauge covers should be removed or secured with duct tape.

If it is at all possible, boats should be removed from the water and stored on land. An MIT study after Hurricane Gloria, found that boats stored ashore were far more likely to survive than boats in the water. If a boat is stored on land it should be well above any possible storm surge and not stored in high-rise storage racks.

You have to prepare for more than the wind. In tidal waters, the storm surge—that sudden rise of water level due to the combination of low pressure and onshore winds—is usually responsible for most of the damage. In addition, open boats must take into account the huge rainfall amounts that accompany hurricanes, nor'easters and thunderstorms. Is your open cockpit self-draining, with nothing loose that can clog the drain? On boats without self-draining cockpits, is the on-board battery charged so that the automatic electric bilge pump can handle the job? Remember also that breaking waves may add to the water in the cockpit. When trying to tend boats in a marina during a hurricane I was bailing water from the cockpit of a small boat with a bucket and couldn't keep up. The boat sank from under me.

Rivers and man-made canals usually provide good "hurricane holes" if the boat must remain in the water. In natural hurricane holes, the shallower the water where the boat is anchored the better, since this provides a better scope ratio for your anchor line. The bottom composition is a great importance, with a sandy bottom giving the best anchor-set. Survey the shoreline around a hurricane hole. If your boat should drag, will it end up on a sandy beach or on the rocks? Boats in canals usually survive better than boats at a marina, provided that they are tied properly and protected from pounding canal bulkheads. A boat kept in the middle of a canal has the best chance—however this requires cooperation from property owners on both sides of the waterway. During hurricane Andrew, one boat owner tied his 26-foot power boat in the center of a canal using eight three-quarter-inch lines, creating a spider web, with his boat as the spider in the center. The boat survived without a scratch. Boats fastened to the bulkheads of canals didn't fare as well, due to pounding from wind and waves. If you plan to moor your boat in the middle of a canal, remember that this can block access to latecomers, so the final tie-up probably cannot be done until the last minute.

Boats secured to a canal bulkhead should employ additional fendering. Usually inflatable fenders just don't do the job, since it's impossible to keep them at the right location, and they frequently collapse from pressure or abrasion. It's a better idea to make up fender boards well in advance, so they can be hung on the sides of the boat to help protect it from pounding. In addition, one or more anchors deployed out into the waterway will help take some of the strain off the fenders.

One of the biggest problems when a boat is kept at a bulkhead or in a marina, is the boat's hull rising above short bulkhead pilings due to the unusually high water level during the storm surge, or from the wave action, or both. When this happens, the boat is frequently impaled on the piling.

In marinas, properly-installed floating docks make fendering and mooring easier. Pilings high enough to be well above the rub-rail of boats during the height of the storm surge are a necessity. Wide slips, with pilings at their outer ends, are also a big advantage in securing a boat that must weather the storm in a marina.

In a slip or at a dock, the bow of the boat should face in the most unprotected, or open-water direction, since this offers the least wind and wave resistance and reduces the chance of waves flooding the cockpit. Boats that have bow-eyes, which are used to winch them up on a trailer, should make use of them as a strong fastening point. Dock-line lengths must be long enough to allow the boat to rise to the maximum expected storm surge (or beyond), and running the mooring lines to the farthest point possible, to allow for this rise, is the rule. Unfortunately, these long line lengths usually mean that a boat in a confined slip has a good chance of rubbing the pilings due to line stretch. Again, fender boards are a big help in this situation.

All cautionary material written about storm survival stresses that you should not try to ride it out on your boat if going ashore is an option. I certainly would not suggest that staying with your boat at a marina—even if allowed—is a good idea. Having said that, I must admit that twice I have done just that.

When Hurricane Belle moved up the east coast in the summer of 1976, I tended the docks at a New Jersey yacht club where my boat was berthed. I adjusted and moved lines on my boat, as well as other boats that I could get to, until the storm surge and waves began washing over the docks. Eventually a half-dozen boats at the yacht club went to the bottom, but my boat survived without a scratch.

Again, in September of 1985, my son, Tom, and I weathered Hurricane Gloria aboard our schooner while in a slip in a marina off Barnegat Bay on the New Jersey coast, tending lines throughout the night. On both of these occasions, line-tending and adjusting prevented our boat from sustaining any damage.

When a big blow is moving your way, large diameter lines should be installed in place of, or in addition to, the normal mooring lines. Nylon mooring lines are the material of choice, since they provide both strength and a shock-absorbing effect to sudden strains. The downside of this shock-absorbing protection is that these nylon lines s-t-r-e-t-c-h. At a mere 200 pounds of pressure, a quarter-inch line, 20 feet long, can stretch 4 feet or more, while under the same pressure, a half-inch line of 20 feet will stretch only about 1 foot. The rule-of-thumb is that a good quality nylon line will stretch 25 percent of its length at 50 percent of its breaking strength. This stretch factor must be taken into account when you are setting up storm lines so that the stretch caused by wind and wave pressure won't allow the boat to pound the dock, the pilings, or an adjoining boat. Remember, larger diameter equals less stretch. Double the diameter and you cut the stretch to one-quarter (the stretch is inversely proportional to the square of the diameter). Also, larger diameter lines are less likely to fail from chafing.

An unexpected finding by MIT after hurricane Gloria showed that many nylon lines that were angled across a chock failed internally when the core melted from the friction created by the repeated stretch-cycles. Most high-quality nylon lines are treated with a lubricant to reduce this type of failure—but this lubricant dissipates with the aging of the line. Another little-known quality of nylon line is that, when wet, it loses about 15 percent of its strength (which returns when the line has dried out). Since we are most concerned with strength during storm conditions—when the line is wet—this is another item to factor into the equation of storm-line size. It's also important to know that for lines of equal diameter, a braided line has more strength than a 3-ply line, and colored line has just slightly less strength than natural.

For those boats that weather a storm on a mooring, there are special considerations. Most yacht clubs and marinas prescribe the equipment used on a permanent mooring, so the underwater portion of a mooring is usually beyond the control of the boat owner. However the pendant, or pendants (pronounced pennants)—and there should be at least two from mooring to boat—should be checked carefully. Since they go through the bow chocks at a sharp angle they are especially subjected to stress and abrasion, and extra chaffing protection is necessary.

This brings us to the question of nylon line quality. There is a wide range of differences in nylon lines, with the cheaper nylon stretching more and having considerably less abrasion resistance and internal lubrication—so don't skimp here. It's much cheaper buying high-quality line than buying a new boat. Insurance companies estimate that up to half of the boat damage from hurricane Andrew, which hit Florida in August 1992, could have been prevented with adequate dock lines.

Unfortunately no matter how well you protect your own boat, frequently it's the careless boat owner near you—whose boat is poorly tied or breaks loose—that can be the cause of your damage. When one boat damages another under these circumstances, insurance companies seldom hold each other liable for damage since they consider it an "Act-of-God" catastrophe. The damage to your boat from the negligence of another owner is the same as if it were your own fault. To help prevent the problem of inadequately tied boats, many marinas and yacht clubs specify minimum line diameters for dock lines. It's a rule designed to counter stupidity. It wouldn't hurt to encourage this policy in all marinas and yacht clubs, and boat owners should see that it is enforced—

for their own protection. A corollary to this rule should be the requirement of larger sized and additional lines when a storm is predicted.

For sailboat owners, there is another consideration. When sailboats are in adjacent slips there is the possibility of their masts and rigging fouling each other as the boats roll "out of sync." These impacts can eventually break the shrouds and drop the mast on deck, in the water, or on another boat. It would be nice if there were always a powerboat in slips between sailboats to prevent this from happening, but it's not a perfect world.

If there is no time to find a snug harbor and your boat has to weather a storm at anchor, the best anchoring-bottom, in descending order of holding, are: sand, clay, hard mud, shells, and soft mud. Needless to say, the larger the anchors and the more anchors deployed, the better. A BoatU.S. test found that embedment type anchors—those that are screwed into the bottom—are the most likely to hold.

We may have a very calm season, but if the Big Blow comes, will you be ready?

The VHF-FM Marine Band

Except for world cruisers, the primary radio communications for small craft is the VHF-FM Marine Band radio, known as a "short range" communications system. It is the communications system of choice for the recreational boater, and a station license from the FCC is no longer required for use within the United States.

VHF stands for Very High Frequency—the band of frequencies between 30 and 300 megahertz (MHz), with wavelengths of 10 to 1 meter, respectively. The Marine Band is located at frequencies between 156 and 163 MHz. This broad VHF band is home to a variety of other services, including FM radio, aviation, police, commercial users such as trucks and taxis, door-openers, scientific and medical users, cordless phones, amateur, radio-control, and television channels 2 through 13. And just like those television signals, this Marine Band is usually described as "line-of-sight,"—so the higher the antenna, the greater the range. (Actually, VHF signals bend slightly, attempting to follow the contour of the earth and, infrequently, when special layers of the ionosphere form a reflective path, they can travel hundreds or thousands of miles).

FM stands for Frequency Modulation—that same type of signal that brings us our FM broadcast stations static free, as well as the sound on our TV.

Although some people new to boating eschew the Marine Band radio in favor of their cell phones, this is not always a good idea, since in an emergency situation, when using the Marine Band, you can reach the Coast Guard directly, and other boaters nearby can also hear your May Day call and come to your assistance. (May Day is a phonetic way for the English-speaking world to say the French phrase, "help me." This term was established in the early part of the last century, before English took over from French as the language of diplomacy and international travel). Cell phones, on the other hand, are an ideal way to communicate with other telephone subscribers on shore for non-emergency calls.

The power of your boat's Marine Band transmitter is limited to a maximum of 25 watts, that is, the amount of radio-frequency energy that goes into the antenna. It is also required that this power can be readily reduced to 1 watt for short range communications.

Antennas for the Marine Band are "vertically polarized." This means that the transmitting antenna element is vertical and, for optimum performance, receiving antennas should also be vertical. (TV antennas, as we have all observed, have horizontal polarization). The "gain" of a Marine Band antenna is a measurement of how much of the antenna's transmit and receive power is concentrated in a desirable direction. Obviously, you don't want to waste power transmitting toward the sky or toward the water, so the "gain" of the antenna is concentrated in a horizontal direction. For sailboats, a gain of 3 dB is the norm, since any higher gain would concentrate the antenna's transmitting and receiving power into an even narrower horizontal beam, which could be counterproductive when a sailboat is heeled. Even for powerboats, too high an antenna gain can result in poor communications when the boat is in rough sea conditions.

On many Marine Band radios you will note that a selection can be made between "International" and "USA." This is because on some channels there is a frequency difference between the two. Thus, for routine communications with the Coast Guard, you must tune to Channel-22 with the American frequency (which is easily remembered by the suffix "A"). Hence, the Coast Guard is listed as Channel 22A. If you were to transmit on the International frequency of Channel-22, the Coast Guard wouldn't hear you since it is a different frequency.

As originally conceived, the Marine Band was relatively simple and straightforward. Channels were allocated for distress, safety and calling, the Coast Guard, commercial vessels, recreational boats, ship-to-ship, ship-to-shore, marine operators (who can connect you into the landline telephone system), and weather.

But the Marine Band is no longer as simple as was originally envisioned. DSC (Digital Selective Calling) technology is now a part of new 25-watt Marine Band radios. Although commercial vessels have had DSC since 1988, it has just recently become available to recreational boaters. With DSC, at the touch of a single button, an automatic May Day call can be transmitted that includes your Maritime Mobile Service Identification Number (MMSI)—which describes your vessel. Also, through an interface with your GPS or Loran, your latitude and longitude can also be automatically transmitted, and these DSC-equipped radios can continue transmitting the emergency message, even when the boat has been abandoned. Unfortunately, in many parts of the country, the Coast Guard is still a couple of years away from having DSC receiving equipment, but many towing companies and yacht clubs can monitor DSC Channel-70, and will relay emergency information to the Coast Guard. The Coast Guard is expected to be fully on-line with DSC by 2006.

DSC can also be used for making direct phone calls without going through the marine operator, or ship-to-ship calls to other DSC-equipped vessels. The sender and designated receiver for these calls, in contrast to non-DSC calls, are private and cannot be monitored by every other boat in the vicinity. When a DSC call is originated, the digital alert signal only takes about a half-second. This half-second signal alerts the designated receiver, usually by a buzzer, and the receiver's screen will show the information as to where and how the message will be sent.

A DSC-equipped radio must be registered with the FCC, which can be easily done through BoatU.S. The MMSI number of each of these radios is similar to a telephone number, so when making a DSC ship-to-ship call, you must know the MMSI number of the other party.

Channel 16 (Ch-16) is the international distress, safety, calling, and reply frequency for vessels and coastal stations. In 1992, in order to relieve congestion on Ch-16, the FCC also designated Channel 9 as the general purpose calling frequency for recreational boats. This is still considered a recommendation, not a requirement. Recreational boats should still make emergency and safety calls on Ch-16.

After an initial contact via Ch-9 or Ch-16, the rest of the contact must be made on another appropriate channel. For example, in an emergency call to the Coast Guard, they will ask you to change to Channel 22A.

Bridge operators monitor Ch-13 and Ch-16 and they also respond to the usual "one long, one short" horn signal—for those without radios aboard. They are generally prompt and cooperative. Many bridges have restricted opening hours. When a call is made for an opening and the bridge operator is unable to comply, he or she will explain the scheduled opening times using Ch-13. A bridge-opening request should be made on low power (1 watt), with the name and location of the bridge along with the name and type of vessel calling, and where they are located. An example might be: "Route-88 bridge, Route-88 bridge, this is the sloop *Happy Days* approaching from the north and requesting a bridge opening."

Another important thing to make note of is the list of VHF-FM weather channels that are available on New Jersey waters:

New York City	WX-1
Holmdel (NW of Manasquan Inlet)	WX-5
Atlantic City	WX-2
Lewes, Delaware	WX-1
Philadelphia	WX-3

Hand-held VHF radios have decreased in size and increased in reliability, and many are now submersible, which makes them great for your "abandon ship" bag. Since most sailboats have their 25 watt, fixed-mount VHF in the cabin, a hand-held can be a great asset in the cockpit, especially when entering a strange marina and receiving directions from the dockmaster, or when talking to a bridge operator. For newer cabin-installed radios there is an alternative: remote microphones that allow channel selection, entire LCD displays, and a speaker, all in the palm of your hand.

New battery technology has also given longer life to hand-helds, with the new nickel metal hydride (NiMH) batteries providing twice as long a time between chargings as the old nickel cadmium rechargeable batteries. However it's still a good idea to keep alkaline batteries in your abandon-ship bag, since they have a shelf life of over five years, whereas a rechargeable battery can self-discharge in a few months.

Cellular Phones and Distress Calls to the Coast Guard

Skippers with cellular phones on board have a special emergency code for contacting the Coast Guard. The call is free of charge, and in New Jersey connects the boater to either the Sandy Hook Station, when calls are made from north of Toms River, or the Cape May Station, when calls are made from south of Toms River. This service is available by dialing: *CG.

One advantage of having a cellular phone over using VHF-FM is the relative privacy it affords—but this privacy can be a negative feature when the phone is used for an emergency at sea. With VHF-FM, there may be other boats nearby that can hear the distress call and come to one's aid, but this is not so when one uses a cell phone. Also, with a cell phone, it is impossible to communicate directly with boats or helicopters involved in a search or rescue mission, whereas, this is possible if one is using VHF Marine Band.

Charts

Throughout this book I've tried to emphasize the importance of up-to-date charts. Nautical charts, at first glance, can be a little intimidating, and they require some study before the navigator feels comfortable using them. NOAA publishes a booklet entitled "Chart No. 1." Chart No. 1 is not a chart at all but rather a small booklet providing all the symbols used on nautical charts; this should be kept on board with one's other charts. Frequently, some, but not necessarily all, of the abbreviations used on the charts can be found on a small table somewhere on the chart itself.

Charts come in a variety of formats and sizes, and they use different types of measuring systems. Intracoastal charts usually measure distance in statute miles; water depths in feet, measured at the average low tide; and bridge clearances in feet, measured at average high tide. Other charts, such as offshore charts, may use nautical miles or fathoms, so it is important to check the key for your chart.

The Mapping Agency in Washington, D.C., has established a number system for charts, which is broken up into geographical areas. For the northeast coast, the chart numbers range from 12,000 to 13,000. For example, one will find that Sandy Hook to Little Egg Harbor is chart #12324.

Every chart also shows the date of issue so that out-of-date charts can be identified and discarded.

The charts that cover New Jersey's coastal and inland waters are

Yonkers to Piermont	#12346
(the Hudson River at the N.J.–N.Y. state line)	
George Washington Bridge to Yonkers	#12345
(the Hudson River south to the G. W. Bridge)	
Day's Point to George Washington Bridge	#12341
(the Hudson River south to Weehawkin)	
Hudson and East Rivers–Governor's Island to 67th Street	#12335
(Lower Manhattan)	
New York Harbor–Upper Bay & Narrows-Anchorage Chart	#12334
(N.Y.'s Upper Bay to south of the Verrazano Bridge)	
New York Lower Bay–Northern Part	#12402
Raritan Bay and Southern Part of Arthur Kill	#12331
Kill Van Kull and Northern Arthur Kill	#12333
Raritan River, Raritan Bay to New Brunswick	#12332
Intracoastal Waterway–Sandy Hook to Little Egg Harbor	#12324
Intracoastal Waterway–Little Egg Harbor to Cape May	#12316
Delaware Bay	#12304
Delaware River–Smyrna River to Wilmington	#12311
Wilmington to Philadelphia	#12312
Philadelphia to Trenton	#12314

Note: A single chart, numbered 12327, covers the same area as charts 12335, 12334, 12402, 12331, and 12333 listed above, but with less detail.

Sales agents for charts, *Tide Tables, Tidal Current Diagrams, Tidal Charts,* and *Coast Pilots* can be found at some marine-supply stores, boat yards, and marinas. Charts and chart books are also available from private publishers, such as: Waterway Guide; BBA; Embassy Coastal Cruising; Home Port Chart, Inc.; Boating Almanac; and several others.

In the last few years electronic chart displays have become a practical alternative for many boaters. These digital charts are displayed on an electronic (usually LCD) screen. Navigational information comes from chart data cartridges, each storing from six to ninety charts, which are based on the NOAA charts. In addition, this system can be coupled with an on-board GPS or Loran that will insert the boat's position directly on to the screen's chart display. Waypoints can also be easily inserted onto the display.

No universal format has yet been established for electronic chart systems, so there are several incompatible systems. The system choice for any of the electronic charts will be determined by the hardware, and there are a wide range of presentations and accessories, depending on the system selected. If electronic charts are used, the skipper must remember that a power-source failure, due to moisture or hardware malfunction, or a nearby lightning strike, can leave the boat without a chart. As with nearly every system on recreational craft, backup, or redundancy, is always important, and the prudent skipper who uses an electronic chart system should also have paper charts on board.

$\mathcal{N}$avigational Instruments

The Compass

Around 1090 AD the Chinese first reported the use of a magnetic needle to indicate north. This primitive compass was an iron needle, magnetized by a lodestone inserted into a straw, and floated in a bowl of water. In Europe, the discovery of the magnetic compass didn't occur until over a century later, in the early 1200s, and historians don't know whether this European discovery was independent or whether it came to them from the Orient. The compass finally allowed thirteenth-century European mariners to determine direction, even under overcast skies or during stormy weather. It was such a simple device, with only one moving part, that it seemed like magic. It was so magical, in fact, that many captains were afraid to use it. It was the age of the Inquisition and sailors feared that if they were seen using this device they could be accused of witchcraft, which could result in torture or death. It wasn't until nearly a century later, during the 1300s, that seamen could finally use the compass openly and without fear.

For the next one hundred years, mariners believed that the compass pointed to true north, but during the 1400s scientists determined that there was a difference between compass north and true north. Finally, in the 1590s, the Portuguese developed surprisingly accurate tables which showed the differences, or *variation*, between true and magnetic north at various places around the globe.

Then, in the 1600s, it was discovered that the magnetic poles changed location from year to year and that the intensity of the magnetic field also varied. Our concepts of a simple magnetic planet were beginning to change.

There are basically two types of magnets: a simple bar magnet, and magnets created by the flow of electricity—electromagnets. In nearly all representations of the earth's magnetic field, the earth's magnet is represented as a simple bar magnet. In reality, the earth's magnetism is more closely related to that of an electromagnet.

The earth's magnetic field is created in the molten iron in the earth's outer core, about 1,850 below the earth's surface, and is influenced to some extent by the solar wind—those charged particles streaming from the sun. The earth's magnetic field is produced by electrical currents that originate in this hot, liquid, outer core of the earth, which is moving around the solid inner core and acting like a huge electromagnet.

The magnetic north pole has been wandering around the polar regions for millions of years. Using data from the 1500s to the present, we see that during this relatively brief period in the history of the earth, the magnetic north pole has made a trip from the Arctic Ocean into northern Canada north of Hudson's Bay, and is now on its way back to the Arctic Ocean north of Alaska at an average speed of about 10 to 15 miles per year. Its speed has increased considerably during the past twenty-five years, and it could just as easily decrease a few years from now.

In addition to the long-term movement of the magnetic poles, there is also a daily (diurnal) movement of the poles. This daily movement of the poles roughly follows an elliptical path around the pole's average position. Sometimes this daily movement follows the path of a very small ellipse, and sometimes a very large one. This can cause the pole to move over 100 miles during a twenty-four-hour period. It's believed that this diurnal movement is caused by the solar wind, and that solar storms on the surface of the sun can cause a change in the size of this elliptic path.

To make things even more confusing, most scientific organizations, such as the American Geophysical Union, consider the term "magnetic pole" to be an over-simplified representation, and prefer to describe at least three different sets of poles, with the "IGRF Model Dip Pole" as the closest to what most cartographers, and the public in general, refer to as the magnetic pole. The difference in angle between magnetic north and true north is called *variation* by mariners.

Although the magnetic lines of force shown around the simple magnets are smooth and regular, the magnetic lines of force around the earth are extremely irregular, primarily due to the nonuniform distribution of magnetic material within the earth. Those erratic lines which show identical variations are known as isogonic lines, and maps are available which show these lines worldwide. But these large-scale maps don't show the many small irregularities that exist locally which, in many cases, can be enormous. Off the Australian coast, for example, there is a position where, in the distance of two football fields, the compass changes by 90 degrees!

There is another bizarre event that occurs with the magnetic poles. About every 250,000 years the poles reverse themselves—the north pole becomes the south pole and vice versa. During the last 5 million years this has happened about twenty-five times. But it has been 780,000 years since this happened the last time, and a reversal is long overdue. However, since the timing of this reversal has always been erratic, it's impossible to tell when it will happen again. Nevertheless, the planet's magnetic field is showing signs of wanting to make the gigantic switch once more. The prelude to this changeover is the gradual weakening of the earth's magnetic field until it becomes zero. Results from measuring the earth's magnetic field in 1980 by the *Magsat* satellite, and in 2000 from the *Orsted* satellite, show a reduction in strength is in progress. When the earth finally becomes nonmagnetic, it will remain that way for possibly several hundred years. Then the magnetism will begin to build up in the opposite direction. For the last 4000 years, this weakening has continued to progress. Just in the past century, the strength of the magnetic field has decreased 5 percent, and scientists predict the earth's magnetic field will cease to exist in a several hundred to a few thousand years—just an instant in geological time.

During the time when the earth is nonmagnetic, compasses, which will point nowhere in particular, will be relegated to museums and children will ask their parents, in awe, "Was the earth once really a magnet?" It's also probable that harmful radiation levels reaching the surface of the earth will increase during this period, when the protection of the magnetic field surrounding the earth has vanished.

Debate has raged among scientists for over 150 years as to how birds, bees, frogs, spiny lobsters, and other creatures are able to consistently and unerringly navigate from one place to another. The latest theory is based on the discovery of a naturally iron-rich substance in their brains, called biogenic magnetite, which can detect magnetic fields.

Perhaps the many centuries it will take for the earth to lose its magnetism will give those migratory animals who navigate using the earth's magnetic field a new way to locate their seasonal destinations.

For the mariner, the nautical chart's compass rose distills all this theoretical information into a convenient, simple, and usable form. The outer ring of the rose shows bearings to the true north pole—the axis of the earth; the next inner ring of the rose shows magnetic bearings—the direction to the magnetic north pole; and on the inside ring is printed the variation, in de-

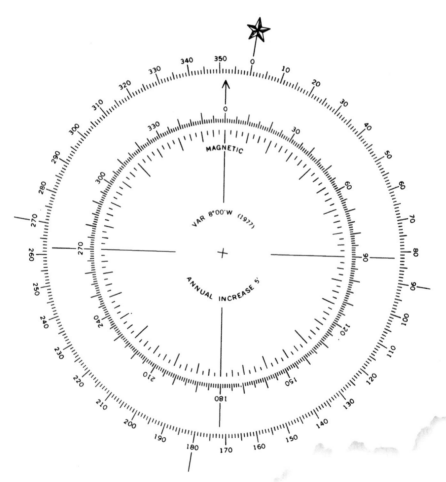

$\mathcal{C}$hart 10.1 The compass rose is on all charts

grees east or west, as well as the annual predicted change in that variation—along with the date that this change was predicted. This yearly predicted change in variation is only applicable for a few years from the date shown since the movement of the magnetic north pole is erratic and unpredictable in the long term.

Although it can be intimidating to reflect on all the changes that are taking place in our magnetic earth, don't throw away your compasses yet! In our lifetime it will still remain as our basic tool for nonelectronic navigation.

More than fifty years ago the gyrocompass made its debut and, more recently, the electronic *fluxgate* compass, with digital or analog liquid crystal display, has taken its place as the latest advancement in compass technology. This new style of compass allows for large, easily read numbers, off-course indicators that utilize bar graphs, remote display capability, automatic deviation correction, and many other features. However because the fluxgate compass is electronic, it is dependent on a supply of electricity, so an old-style compass is still a good backup to have aboard.

The "swinging" of a compass, that is, adjusting the compensators on the compass to remove as much of the error as possible, has been greatly simplified since the advent of accurate GPS readouts of true course.

Radar

Radio Detecting and Ranging is better known by its acronym RADAR, and has been in practical use since World War II. The first experiments were made by Guglielmo Marconi, the father of radio. The system determines distance and azimuths from the transmitted pulses of high-frequency radio signals that are reflected by the targets—other boats, buoys, land masses, buildings, bridges, and so on, or by *transponders*, which emit their own radar signal when prompted by another radar. The same antenna is used for the transmit and receive pulses, and the time it takes for the signal to make the round trip is timed and used for the screen display.

In recent years, small-craft radars have been considerably reduced in size, power requirements, and price, while their on-screen programs and interface capabilities have expanded. Now, most units use LCD screens (liquid crystal display), which replaced the more cumbersome and power-hungry CRTs (cathode ray tubes) of the past. All modern units now use raster display (just like your TV set) rather than the rotating display of previous years. This greatly improves the ease of operation. The ability of a radar unit to network with other electronic gear on board, such as Loran, autopilot, GPS, or electronic charts, is an important consideration when purchasing a new one. This ability of various different pieces of equipment to talk the same language is termed the "protocol." When interfacing is planned, be sure the separate units will be able to use the same protocol. The type of antenna, the beam width, the range, and the antenna placement are also important concerns that should be discussed before the purchase is made and the installation completed.

Loran-C

LORAN, an acronym for Long Range Navigation, has until recently been the system of choice for determining a small boat's position in coastal waters. Although it is still operational, it has become almost completely supplanted by GPS, and stores and catalogs no longer list Loran units for sale. GPS, the satellite Global Positioning System, is now the small-boat navigation gear of choice, and its price has dropped to well below the price of Loran, while its accuracy is much greater. During the Radionavigation Users Conference in 1993, the Commander of the U.S. Coast Guard suggested that, due to the success of the GPS system, it would be technically and economically justified to terminate Loran-C, which would save the Coast Guard an estimated $25 million a year.

The Loran receiver develops its fixes from powerful low-frequency land-based transmitters scattered along the coast as well as inland. By measuring the time differences of the signals received from these stations (TDs), the units give readouts either of these TD lines (shown on many charts) or of a latitude and longitude conversion, accomplished through complex algorithms within the Loran receiver. Since the TD lines are hyperbolas, the system is called a hyperbolic navigational system.

GPS, DGPS, and WAAS

In October 1957, the first man-made satellite was thrust into orbit around the earth. The USSR's tiny *Sputnik* had beaten the United States into space. The U.S., in an effort to learn as much about *Sputnik* as possible, monitored the beeping signal it transmitted, and was able to determine its location through the Doppler effect. This was the genesis of using man-made satellites to determine navigational information. But it wasn't until the 1970s that the satellite navigation system, as we now know it, began to take shape.

Satellite navigation began in the mid 1960s with the U.S. Navy's NAVSAT system (an acronym for Navy Satellite). It was based on the same Doppler shift phenomenon used to track *Sputnik*. Doppler shift is the apparent change in wavelengths as the distance between the source and the receiving station increases or decreases. This is the same effect that is heard when a car horn or a train whistle changes from a higher to a lower pitch as it goes by.

The second generation satellite navigation system, the one now available to recreational boaters, is known as the NAVSTAR Global Positioning System, or simply GPS. The Global Positioning System (GPS) is a satellite navigation system that was designed for and is operated by the U.S. military, but it is now used by millions of civilians worldwide. The basic space segment of this system, known as the "GPS Operational Constellation," consists of twenty-four satellites that orbit the earth twice a day; however there are often more than twenty-four in space, as new ones are placed in orbit to replace those whose on-board fuel has become exhausted.

There are six separate satellite orbits, usually with four satellites traveling in each of these orbital paths. These orbits are spaced around the equator 60 degrees apart, and their orbital planes are canted about 55 degrees to the equatorial plane. Thus, this GPS constellation configuration provides the user at any point on earth with five or more visible satellites at any time. With access to just three satellites, a two-dimensional fix (latitude and longitude) can be determined; and with four satellites, GPS receivers can compute a location in three dimensions. This makes the GPS navigation system ideal for aircraft, as well as for boats, ground transportation, and hikers. Every GPS receiver has an inexpensive built-in clock—about the same as a quartz wristwatch. Each GPS satellite contains an atomic clock. When a satellite is acquired by the GPS receiver, it locks the receiver's inexpensive clock into the satellite's atomic time. Then by measuring the time interval between the transmission and reception of a satellite signal, a spherical "line-of-position" is created around each satellite.

Every type of navigation system makes use of lines of position. These lines of position may be a straight line, curved lines, a section of a circle, parabolic, or in the case of GPS, spheres. The intersection of lines of position in any navigational system determines your location, and in GPS it is the intersection of these spheres.

GPS satellites transmit in the microwave spectrum. At these frequencies the wavelength is very short and the receiving antenna can consequently be very small. One of the problems with this frequency is that it does not easily pass through things like house roofs, cabin tops, or people (if you're holding a hand-held GPS at waist height, the receiver has difficulty acquiring a satellite from the other side of your body).

When initially put into service, the GPS system was so accurate, that the Department of Defense deliberately introduced an error into the civilian GPS system to prevent its use by terrorists. However this error, called Selective Availability (SA), caused a potential hazard to users. If a boat were coming through a narrow inlet in a fog, the error that was introduced by Selective Availability could put the boat on the rocks. So the Coast Guard established low-frequency AM ground stations along the coast. Accessing the data from one of these Coast Guard stations would take out the error introduced by the Department of Defense. This system, Differential GPS (DGPS), requires a separate antenna system and receiver, which is frequently more expensive than the GPS receiver itself. Finally, in May 2000, the Selective Availability error was discontinued, and overnight GPS users worldwide had a dramatically more accurate system.

However there were still potential errors in the system—such as clock errors, ionospheric and tropospheric delays as the signal travels from the satellites to earth, earth reflections, satellite orbital drifts, and control errors—and the DGPS ground stations' corrections could reduce most of these errors. But those ground stations, which required the separate receiver and antenna, had limited range, and were subject to noise and fading, so geostationary satellites, operating in the same frequency band as the GPS satellites, were put in orbit, and these new "stationary" satellites provide corrections that can be received directly on a GPS antenna without the need of a separate receiver and antenna system. This improved correction system is known as the Wide Area Augmentation System (WAAS).

As improvements continue, consumer prices for GPS receivers keep dropping, while accuracy, operational simplicity, and extra features are expanding. GPS receivers have the ability to "talk" to other electronic equipment on board, such as an electronic chart plotters, autopilot, VHF-FM radio, radar, etc. But in order to carry on their conversation, they must be talking the same language. The current protocol (as of this writing) is "NMEA 0183."

GPS and units that combine a GPS and chart plotter, have a very small battery drain, and provide today's sailor with navigational capabilities undreamed of a few decades ago.

Networking of Navigational Equipment

When electronic navigational equipment first began proliferating on small boats, the individual systems had no way of exchanging information. Early equipment manufacturers, lacking universal interface language, developed proprietary languages within each company to tie equipment together. This lack of a universal electronic language was bad for consumers, since it prevented mixing equipment from different manufacturers. Finally, in 1979, the National Marine Electronics Association (NMEA) began drafting an interface protocol, and in 1980 the NMEA 0180 format was adopted.

The NMEA 0180 was a relatively simplistic system, and the rapid progression of marine electronics required more flexibility—which was provided by the NMEA 0183 format (adopted in 1983) that went on to become an international standard. But even this system does not provide a language adaptable enough for the rapid growth in marine electronics, and newer versions of NMEA 0183 are now being developed.

Marine Sanitation Devices

With the increased population density near our coastal waters as well as the burgeoning boating population that uses these waters, sewage disposal both along the shore and on the water has become crucial. The regulations governing sewage discharge from boats in U.S. waters went into effect in 1980 and have not changed appreciably since then. Basically, the law says that beyond 3 miles offshore a direct pumpout of untreated sewage is allowed (but discouraged). Within 3 miles of shore, and for the intracoastal waters, sewage that has been treated with a Coast Guard approved marine sanitation device (MSD) may be discharged. The only exception to the use of an MSD within the 3 mile limit and in intracoastal waters is when an area has been designated as a No Discharge Zone (NDZ). In a specified NDZ, even sewage that has been treated with a Coast Guard approved on-board treatment system is not allowed to be discharged. If a vessel has an installed head (rather than a porta-potty), it must have an operable Coast Guard certified marine sanitation device. There are three types of MSDs:

Type I: The Type I MSD chemically treats and macerates the sewage and is required to reduce the bacteria count to under 1,000 per 100 ml of discharge. The Type I MSD is acceptable for all boats less than 65 feet long. Raritan's ElectrSan and Sealand's SanX are the two most common Type I MSDs on the market. They reduce the bacteria count to far less than the maximum allowed—in fact these type of on-board sewage treatment systems are usually about one hundred times better than a municipal treatment plant.

Type II: Type II MSDs use a similar process to the Type I MSDs but adhere to stricter standards. They allow no more than 1,000 parts of any suspended matter per 100 ml, and their wastewater discharge is almost clear. All boats longer than 65 feet must have a Type II MSD. These MSDs provide treatment that is usually one thousand times better than a municipal system.

Type III: A Type III MSD is a holding tank (a porta-potty is a Type III MSD). Type III is the only MSD acceptable in all waters. Their disadvantage is that the holding tank takes up lots of room and has to be pumped out frequently—and often pump-out stations are hard to find.

Depending on the restrictions of the particular waters you are in, the acceptable on-board system has to be "locked in place." That is, valves that are in the correct position must have a clamp or padlock. There should also be a placard posted that specifies the restrictions of sewage disposal. If you fail to observe these rules and are boarded for inspection, the result could be a hefty fine.

Reference Material

Although navigational equipment and charts provide a boater's basic requirements, there are many other sources of information available to the recreational boater, both in print as well as in less traditional formats.

New Jersey State Police—Boating Safety is a booklet containing the regulations for recreational boaters that are specific to the New Jersey boater. It is a "must have" that can be obtained from the New Jersey Marine Police directly, or at their booths in many of the local boat shows.

Navigation Rules is published by the Coast Guard and details the rules of the road in both text and pictorial displays. It is also "must" reading and should be kept on board as a reference.

The United States Coast Pilot is a government publication that features comprehensive, up-to-date, easy-to-follow listings of opening times for every bridge, as well as listings of lights, buoys, sound signals, day-beacons, RACONS, radio beacons, navigational information, and other aids to navigation maintained by or under the authority of the U.S. Coast Guard. The publication includes illustrations of aids to navigation and a glossary of terminology relating to these aids. Separate volumes are printed for each geographical area and may be obtained from the superintendent of documents, U.S. Government Printing Office, or from dealers of government charts.

Chapman's Piloting, Seamanship, and Small Boat Handling has been the bible of recreational boaters for several decades. As the name implies, it covers all phases of seamanship and is an excellent reference book covering all topics of interest to the small boat skipper.

Waterway Guide is a yearly publication that gives a detailed description of small-craft marinas and their services along the Intracoastal Waterway from Canada to the Mexican border. It is published in several editions. The *Waterway Guide, Northern Edition* covers New Jersey's waters as well as the coastal and intracoastal waters between the Canadian border and the Delmarva Peninsula.

*T*hese are just a few of the myriad publications and electronic information services available. Depending on the cruise intended, other periodicals to consider might include, *Tide and Current Tables, Coastal Loran Coordinates*, and *Eldridge*. In recent years there have also been a large number of videos available, covering all topics ranging from marine engine repair to "cruising into the sunset," which many people find appealing.

⚓ Index

When the state name is not included in the listing, the location is in New Jersey.

⚓ ⚓

About the Author

Captain Don Launer is a lifetime resident of New Jersey. He now lives in Forked River, on the shore of Barnegat Bay, on the state's central Atlantic coastline. He has held a U.S. Coast Guard captain's license for more than twenty-five years and is a frequent contributor to boating magazines and newspapers, most notably *Cruising World* magazine, *Offshore* magazine, *SAIL* magazine, and the Jersey shore newspaper *The Beachcomber.* He was field editor for the yearly publication *Waterway Guide* for fifteen years, and is now Contributing Editor of *Good Old Boat Magazine.*

Over the years he has cruised New Jersey's waters extensively, while on vacation and doing boat deliveries. He has also cruised the entire east coast from Canada to the Florida Keys, and he has skippered charters in the Bahamas, the Virgin Islands, and the Mediterranean.

The author, Captain Don Launer

In what he likes to call his "previous life," he worked in commercial television at ABC-TV in New York City, traveling the world to cover the Olympic Games. His work won him two Emmy Awards.

In addition to his captain's license, Don holds a General Class FCC license, the highest of the commercial radio licenses; an Amateur Radio Operator's license; and a private pilot's license for single-engine land and sea.

As a member of the Barnegat Baywatch program, sponsored by the Alliance for a Living Ocean, he does water quality monitoring of Barnegat Bay's waters twice a month during the boating season.

Don has been on or around the water all his life. As a child he spent his summers in Lavalette, on the New Jersey shore, or camping along the upper Delaware River, where his brother, Philip, and he would explore the waters in a variety of small craft.

Before World War II his family frequently spent summers in Europe. These shipboard crossings, along with those he took when in the armed forces during the war, combine to make a dozen Atlantic Ocean crossings.

His earliest memory as a child took place on the water—during a nearly disastrous experience.

When he was about five years old, his mother was returning from Europe with him and his brother. A couple of days before arriving in New York City, the ship blundered into a late-summer hurricane that was rapidly moving up the coast. At that time hurricanes could not be tracked or forecast. Portholes were smashed, and at each roll of the ship, water poured through them. In their cabin, water was 2 or 3 feet deep. Their mother tied them into the upper bunk. The ship almost didn't make it, and when it arrived in New York, there was a long line of ambulances waiting for the passengers with broken bones and head injuries.

It didn't seem to dampen Don's enthusiasm for being on the water. He has owned his own boat since he was eleven years old, and has frequently had more than one at a time. He owns six at this writing, and he's owned more than eighteen during his lifetime. Many of them he built himself.

He met his wife, Elsie, in the 1940s while he was working as a lifeguard. They have two children, and the entire family loves the water. Don's daughter, Kathy, windsurfs, scuba dives, and enjoys going out in her father's schooner—especially when small-craft warnings are up.

Kathy has carried the tradition to her own family. She taught her two daughters, Jennifer and Nancy, to swim before they could walk. They're completely at home in and around the water.

Don's son, Tom, owns a sailboat and also enjoys his father's schooner, which he helped him build. Tom has been sailing with his father since he was two years old, and he had his own boat when he was four.

Now semi-retired, Captain Launer cruises the East Coast in his two-masted schooner *Delphinus* and gunkholes in his sailing dinghy or his kayak.